INHABITING INTERDEPENDENCE

Also by John Bloom

SAUCY TOMATOES AND BLUEBERRY THRILLS
A Humorous Harvest from the Biodynamic Farm
(SteinerBooks, 2014)

SLOW INVESTING
How Your Money Can Transform the World (editor)
(Lilipoh, 2012)

THE GENIUS OF MONEY
Essays and Interviews Reimagining the Financial World
(SteinerBooks, 2009)

PHOTOGRAPHY AT BAY
Interviews, Essays, and Reviews
(University of New Mexico, 1993)

INHABITING
INTERDEPENDENCE

being in the next economy

John Bloom

SteinerBooks | 2016

2016
SteinerBooks
An imprint of Anthroposophic Press, Inc.
610 Main Street, Great Barrington, MA 01230
www.steinerbooks.org

Book and cover design: Jens Jensen
Cover image: *The Shape of Intuition*
All images are © copyright by the author
except photo of Martin Luther King, Jr., Memorial
© copyright by M. Dogan.
Images used by permission.

LIBRARY OF CONGRESS CONTROL NUMBER 2016944762

ISBN: 978-1-62148-175-1 (paperback)
ISBN: 978-1-62148-176-8 (eBook)

CONTENTS

ASSOCIATIVE ECONOMIC TRANSACTIONS

LAND AND MONEY

ACKNOWLEDGEMENTS

These essays were written from 2008 through 2015, essentially since the publication of my earlier book *The Genius of Money* published in 2009. I have chosen to include one essay from that book as it held many of the thematic seeds that emerged in subsequent years. In support of my pulling together this collection, I have many people to appreciate. In particular I would like to mention Joan Caldarera, my wife and talking partner, who asked the hard questions, challenged the framing, and offered suggestions for moving through impasses in thinking and language.

I would also like to thank RSF Social Finance, my colleagues and former colleagues there, who provided reflections on the content, and have given me editorial comment, and the gift of time to reflect.

Without the spiritual and financial support of the AnJel Fund at RSF, this book would not have come about. The advisors to the fund have been deeply engaged in the topics covered, and they have made possible the conditions to write many of these pieces.

Of course, there is no end to transforming the way the world works with money. Thus, appreciation for Don Shaffer, President & CEO of RSF Social Finance, who first formulated RSF's fourfold theory of change—that all financial transactions are direct, transparent, personal, and based on long-term relationships. This framework is enough in itself to challenge every assumption of our current financial system. Much of what I have written here could be an application of that proposition, while the inspiration of Rudolf Steiner's vision of the human being and the threefold social commonwealth continue to enliven and challenge my thinking. In some ways these essays could be considered a kind of continuing research into our future social being.

John Bloom
San Francisco, 2016

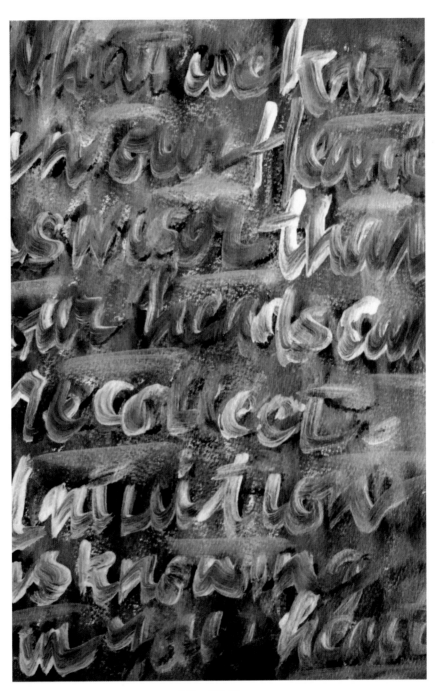

What We Know

INTRODUCTION

O ld habits die hard—habits of mind, heart, and deed. So if we are to inhabit an interdependent economy, it will be as much about dying and falling away as it is about emergence and maturation. What stands behind this thought is the image of molting, one of those magical natural processes that has the power to inspire wonder and at the same time carry a whole story of adaptation and regeneration. It also serves as a cogent metaphor for where we are and what is needed in the evolution of economic consciousness.

In the animal world, the process of molting is one visible indicator of a deeper and more longitudinal metamorphosis. What the process leaves behind is the exuviae, mineral matter of what once served as a kind of boundary between the being of the animal and the rest of the world. The actual moment of molt, when the animal moves out of the residual shell, marks the transition moment between the old and the next, between that which has outlived its service and that which has been generated to serve in the next stage. Such a moment is also one of great vulnerability. The new skin still fresh has yet to harden into its protective state. It is a moment predators seek. As the lessons of nature and time indicate, return to the old is not possible. And, if a molting species fails to molt, it will not survive.

So it is risky to say that a metaphor can be predictive since it is nothing more than an invention of mind, but it is also unwise to underestimate the power of image and imagination as a kind of guide for reframing what and how we know. If anyone desires to move out of our aging unjust and ecologically self-destructive economy, then the inner metamorphic work, self-transformation, is absolutely essential to preparing a molt that marks a change of consciousness that will in turn serve our interdependent economic world in a way that is future bearing and sensitive to the needs of all. So molt we must, but with a cautionary awareness that the human mind, in its wish or need for power, security, and fear of change, can recreate the old and call it new. The animal kingdom carries no such consciousness—it serves instead as teacher and metaphor holder for what is truly a human challenge. How can we step into an interdependent economy with a new conscious-ness? What has to be unlearned, reconsidered, reappraised? And what assumptions about our individual and organizational oper-ating systems have to be dissolved? And what are the new ones?

This collection of essays is concerned with finding and fram-ing new assumptions that support how each of us shows up in an interdependent economy. It is meant to serve those who have or are coming to the conclusion that something is radically wrong with the current state of economic affairs in which inequality and environmental degradation have taken on an oppressive presence in daily life.

In the spirit of emergence, and with yearning for a bold molt releasing a new economic consciousness, these essays are noth-ing more than a guide to reimagining money and economic life. They are tools for the work each of us can do on ourselves out of a sense for the commonwealth of humanity. The forces resisting change are manifold and strong, and predators seek the vulner-able. So we need each other and an awareness of the reality of our economic interdependence to push through change and to flour-ish. Transformation begins with questioning authority, question-ing assumptions. And, I hope I have done that effectively. But inquiry itself is no longer enough. If we are to molt, it means tak-ing authority, knowing why and toward what end, and then using that authority for the wellbeing of all. The purpose of these essays, ordered on the themes of the next economy, work, organizations, money and spirit, economic associations, and land, is to support the development of new thinking and practical approaches—to inspire inhabiting an interdependent economy—even if it is one person at a time.

1

HEART'S GUIDANCE

An Economic Imagination

The mind thinks it loves;
the heart loves before the thought.

In our current stage of materialist economy, we are entranced with capital and disconnected from our hearts. This discord is a result of the inherent nature of capital, so centered as it is in the head, as the origin of the word indicates. In the visible world discord looks like a widening gap between wealth and poverty, and in the inner world like a disintegration of beliefs, values, and behavioral decisions. Make no mistake, we need capital in one form or another, *and* we need those who work with capital to be in the world in a way that values each human being and supports the regeneration of nature. This inner integrity might then begin to heal social and ecological wounds.

So, how might the imagination of economic life change from where we currently are—dependence on growth that is heading toward the demise of nature and increased suffering—to one that is instead life affirming and regenerative? The purpose of this essay is to focus on a guiding framework for systemic change. Real change never happens without a guiding imagination.

Let's start with the basics. As I remember, the things that I needed to know or commit to memory, I learned by heart—a poem, a lifeline phone number, a lover's birthday. I suspect this is true for others as well, though ever-present reference technology has helped us grow lazy about such matters. Long before textbooks, encyclopedias, and Wikipedias, the heart is what we had by way of stored knowledge, even while it was the head's task to process that knowledge. Thus, consciousness has been as much if not more a product of the heart than of the head, though modern industrial culture has come to prize intellect over character. We have learned how to perceive and transform nature, while also learning from each other in order to survive as individuals and in communities.

As we evolved, our relationships were practical as well as spiritual; that is to say that trust catalyzed community action, whether the trust was a result of blood connection or common cause. Each individual discovers and develops her or his own capacities or gifts. And, it is when those capacities begin to serve both self and others that glimmerings of economic life emerge. Fast forward and you get the industrialized version of economic efficiencies in the division of labor. When I am contributing my capacities and in return receiving what I need back from the community, I feel engaged, recognized, and valued—supported both materially and through a sense of fulfillment. While this is a somewhat simplistic framing, I believe this feeling is one desired not only by me, but also by a significant number of individuals open to reflecting on the nature of vocation and economic life.

What I am describing is a heart-centered economy, one motivated by continuous circulation, connection, caring, and cognizant of each person's dignity and destiny. And most important, an economy in which the rediscovery of trust becomes the vital element supporting the circulation and regeneration of resources as common, co-produced wealth, including but certainly not limited to money. After all, money emerged primarily as an economic convenience, as a portable way to store value. By agreement its value was established through the exchange of goods and services. It was a means. But, as money has become more a valued commodity in and of itself, it has been disconnected from its purpose of accounting for economic flow, disconnected from real needs and human activity. In this sense, the more money is valued as an accumulated object attached to an individual, the more antisocial it becomes. In contrast, economics is deeply social as we are fully dependent upon one another's capacities to meet our material needs.

As an organ, the human heart plays a leading role in maintaining human life forces. And, it works in a fully integrated system. It is an arbiter between the intense circulatory exchange in the fine capillaries at the extremities and need for constant vertical movement as the blood moves through the heart's chambers. Blood, exhausted after delivering its nutrients along the way to the periphery, returns to the heart–lung center to be revitalized—a systolic, diastolic rhythm of constant exchange. There is no part of the human organism that is not permeated through circulation, and just about any stoppage in that circulation has significant health consequences. I am certainly not the first to use the circulation of blood as simile for the circulation of money. This is an illuminating but partial picture. Circulation is meaningless without the management capacities of the heart, its sensitivity to our inner and outer-facing nerve–sense system, and the forces of our metabolic system. Simply put, the heart embodies interdependence, serves as guide and guardian, harmonizer for human life, and thus supports our capacities to think and act. This complete and unalterable interdependence has much to tell us about economic life.

How the heart models service is in stark contrast to dominance of self-interest, a concept intractably nestled in the modern evolution of economic thinking. Self-interest as currently fostered and practiced has become debased from the moral, and I would say religious, framework that says that it is in your self-interest to be interested in and help others. As economic experience has become increasingly embedded in the materialism and consumerism of the marketplace, interest in the other has converted into competitive fear of those others. Money is the measure of the human being; thus, I am better the more I can extract from the system for myself. This is a powerfully destructive thought.

It is fascinating to me to consider that the heart is naturally moral. It does not deny one part of the body over another unless it needs to allocate healing resources for an interim period. It does not judge, it simply recognizes need and responds. It seeks sufficiency, and its actions are all guided by the impulse to restore balance—all for the purposes of circulation and meeting the needs of the whole throughout a very diverse organic system. Many natural systems are like this. Nature is moral, but somehow we have allowed the antisocial power of money to corrupt this moral element in human nature. It doesn't feel right. Just as self-interest gives the lie to how truly interdependent we are, money supports the illusion of independence and serves as a measure of fittest in the Darwinian notion of survival. If the money was won through competition, what was lost along the way? These are not propositions of the heart. They are propositions of the head; rationalizations for historical patterns, and cynically, justifications for essentially immoral behavior in the financial marketplace. The heart does not speculate, it anticipates and regulates, not as an exercise in control, but rather in service to the whole.

So what is capital, and how does it serve in the heart imagination? One could say that capital is the materialization of spirit, spirit brought into matter through economic activity. This may seem a stretch, but consider the following. Economic life evolves from the work it takes to transform natural resources into practical goods. Of course, the transformation is not magical, rather it is often hard won through trial and error, through the application of physical and mental creative powers. The invention and evolution of the plow, or any machine for that matter, demonstrates the additive, transformative power of applied consciousness across generations and geography. A second development is how these powers are harnessed and organized for efficiency and production through the further application of intelligence. This applied intelligence in combination with the production of goods and services is what gives rise to capital.* Capital is to the economic realm what intelligence is to the individual. Since intelligence is not material, that is, it has no physical substance, it is by its nature nonobjective. Its value appears as practical activity in the world. Capital is spiritual, while its value, its measure, derives from its application at a specific time and place.

The role of capital in the heart economy is like that of oxygen to the human heart. Oxygen is carried through the blood even as that stream is also collecting the carbon dioxide waste, which it returns to the world through breath. This self-regenerative system is the key to the imagination of a heart-centered economy.

I offer this imagination as a starting point for changing how we think about and live our economic life through our daily transactions. Can we see that we are part of a great circulation? Can we see that we are part of both the destruction and regeneration of natural systems, and that in our economic world we are never separate from each other, from wealth or poverty of resources, even though we have been conditioned to think that way? If, in our own body system, we were to establish "political" boundaries and protect them as we do, we would die an instant death. Boundaries are important, just as cell membranes are important. They are permeable; they protect, and contain, but in the end it is the circulation that is the most vital. And it is the workings of the human heart, the servant of the circulatory system that demonstrates the wisdom we need to transform money, the financial system, and economic life. Not only *by*, but also *from* the heart we can learn how the world can support our lives as we work consciously to support others.*

---

*   This chapter was inspired by Rudolf Steiner's insights into economics. In his 1922 lecture cycle, now published under the title *Rethinking Economics: Lectures and Seminars on World Economics*, he goes into great depth on how these two essential capacities, labor and intelligence, create value.

Untitled

FROM CO-CREATION TO ASSOCIATION

A Social Challenge for the Next Economy

S earch the term *co-creation* on the Internet, and you will find it described primarily as a marketing technique. A company puts out a product, opens the lines of communication with its consumers and shapes the products based upon the input. This level of invitation is made possible by the immediacy of digital feedback loops and the emerging abilities of manufacturers to customize products. This loop becomes self-reinforcing once the consumers see their ideas implemented and become more tightly wound with the product or brand. There are multiple benefits to this particular co-creative marketing approach, perhaps the most important of which is the reduction of unnecessary and wasteful production. Such an approach is an important step forward from an environmental perspective; yet, this view of co-creation is mostly driven by market share through customer loyalty. Much more than market value is possible through co-creation. If practiced as a community, it can serve as the basis for coauthoring significant portions of economic life, and at the same time re-inspire participation in civil society.

In the study of human creativity, problem solving is a distinct research subset simply because it has a beginning, middle and end, and can be observed in a laboratory. From the standpoint of research, such a neat package makes for measurable outcomes and publishable data. However, if all of our creative thinking were framed around problems–solutions, we'd all be in full-time analysis. Consider instead, the deeper creative processes of imagination, inspiration, and intuition. While they are all at work in our daily lives, they are much harder to grasp. Some simple working definitions are in order. Imagination is the capacity to form recognizable and plastic pictures, and for those pictures to transform through experiencing others'. Inspiration is that energy we breathe in that renews a sense of what is possible. Intuition is the capacity to know without knowing, to know through direct experience without the intellectual or cultural constructs of thinking. These are simplifications of very complex processes, and these "i" words are often misused in popular culture. Further, in some spiritual traditions they have very specific even sacred meanings, and, though I am trying to craft some basic practical concepts, I do so with respect for their spiritual heritage. They are capacities that one can develop only for oneself, and as one develops them one can come to recognize those capacities in others.

Imagination, inspiration, and intuition are capacities rather than outcomes, techniques of knowing rather than ends in themselves. They function most effectively in context of trust, and least effectively in a context of analysis and doubt. Yet they frequently inform, even if unconsciously, problem solving and other forms of decision making, despite the dominant Western culture's predisposition to have faith or comfort in more "rational" processes.

It is challenge enough for each of us to understand how the capacities of imagination, inspiration, and intuition are at work in each of our lives, and they are present, and sometimes more heightened, when participating in a group. Yet, something new is possible within and through a group that could not be possible for an individual. For example, how many times have you sat in a group that was struggling to see a way forward whatever the situation, when an idea arose that no one person in the group had originally thought of? Where did the idea come from? How could we understand this process as co-creative? I am describing a process in which imagination, inspiration, and intuition are operating as a group capacity, operating in a way that recognizes individual capacities, yet transcends them. I would hold that understanding this collectively evolved consciousness, the reality that we co-create with others, is a critical, if difficult to achieve, practice needed for transforming our economic relationships. Imagination, inspiration, and intuition are essential "tools" for understanding not only ourselves but also others with whom we create our interdependent communities.

Co-creation is not some far-fetched idealistic notion. There are long-standing and deep traditions of practice from which to learn, such as Native American Councils and the Quaker Meeting, and more recent ones such as Chaordic Organizations, Goethean Conversation, and Theory U. All these practices acknowledge some spiritual background or presence, and the work is to open as a group to what voice may emerge from silence, deep listening, and attendance to the emergent. These are group wisdom practices that foster and result from imagination, inspiration, and intuition. And these practices are one way of accessing spiritual guidance in organizational decision-making. They are not to be taken lightly or used superficially.

One important aspect of co-creation is that while it calls for each person's highest self, our better nature, it is not a democratic form. Co-creation recognizes the unique capacities and perspectives each person brings to a circle, and eliminates the polarizing affect of competition for power. A decision, or the sense of the group, is a shared emergent experience rather than a voting process in which everyone has to agree. One could say in contrast to the democratic that co-creation is more of a republican form (in the vein of Plato's *Republic*) in which the strength of each person is present within collective imagination of community, and that each person carries within a sense of responsibility for the whole community.

As with co-creation, an economy is also not a democratic form, but rather a more republican one. An economy thrives out of real interdependence, recognizing the gifts we bear and material needs we have. If our long-term aim is to evolve into an associative economy, which in its simplest form brings together producers, distributors, and consumers to set prices, then learning to recognize the importance of co-creative processes and to discipline ourselves to work within them is a critical step along that path. An associative economy will not evolve without the parallel social transformation made real through co-creation.

3

REFLECTIONS ON INEQUALITY

There are only so many ways to describe the widening gap between the wealthy and the poor. No one seems to disagree that the gap exists, and no one seems to question that the defining element of it is money and all that accrues to it. Also no question, the whole financial resource terrain looks and feels quite different depending upon where one stands in it with material assets, a belief system, or philosophical worldview. If one views the wealth gap as a problem, it is clear there is no simple fix. If I have already lost you, here is a radical counter-imagination: What if one were to consider love as the defining element of wealth, and further "account" for how much we need and experience the supporting flow of it? This wealth gap might look quite different than the monetary one. So it is important and central to my purpose to determine what problem is worth solving if the intention is one of peace and shared earth. Wealth is a good thing; it makes many things possible. On one level we produce it by simple interest in and care for others. On another, money could be viewed as the holder of collectively produced economic value. That is the light side of money. The shadow: That money is considered as owned, treated as a commodity, and driven by self-interested behavior is one expression of a much bigger and challenging materialistic world view that has lost sight of resource sufficiency and economic interdependence, while fostering cultural exclusion and isolation of the individual.

As others do, I struggle with the extremity of the wealth situation from both moral and practical perspectives. The circumstances feel unjust and disastrous for all given the continued extraction and over-accumulation of wealth from the financial system and the continued commodification of land, labor, and capital. Just as there are ecological limits so, too, are there limits to suffering—and as a society in general we seem to have turned a blind eye to both. Thus I am challenged to find the ground on which to stand that might provide a foundation for transforming the unhealthy, unsustainable, and disempowering tendencies of our time. Although I know that there are groups actively working on aspects of this transformation, I find myself in a stuck place unable to step outside my privilege or adequately into others' disadvantage.

I want to be clear that I am in that stuck place both outwardly in the work that I do with money and organizations, and inwardly with knowing that there are barriers to my speaking with convincing solidarity to others' oppression, internalized oppression, or invisibility. At the same time, I know that both privilege and oppression are bound in the same system of which I am a part. In my attempt to free myself from this dilemma long enough to explore the great wealth divide, or at least imagine I can do so, I would ask forbearance and forgiveness from those who bristle at what I am trying to address and how I address it, simply because I am not one of them. I know of no other way through my morass except to take such a risk and invite anyone else struggling with these issues to participate in a way that opens inclusive dialogue.

Much has been written about the topic of inequality—its origins in a capitalist system, in greed, in political power and policy, in control of natural resources, in cultural dominance, in winning and self-worth measured by wealth. Rarely is the value of human capacities celebrated beyond the statistical framework of productivity. However, the telltale facts of the great balance sheet remain regardless of the lens through which one looks. Given the current state of affairs, solutions such as a universal tax on wealth, or a transformation of the capital system away from the rule of owning class, are a virtual stalemate. Inviting those who are at an advantage to relinquish that advantage is a strategy sure to fail. Inviting those at a disadvantage to the path of insurrection is also a failing approach. The path of nonviolent transformation is slow and enervating. And, naming a problem doesn't change it.

I would argue that inequality represents a spiritual or moral crisis, which reaches beyond class, beyond political boundaries, beyond identity, beyond the behavior of any individual, though this is where change can start. This crisis is not about the possession or dispossession of material resources—these are no more than indicators, byproducts or painful reminders of a deeper systemic issue. Wealth is a natural phenomenon; it is the result of economic activity. How that wealth is treated, used, or owned is another matter that bespeaks the state of human nature. From this perspective, when we value money and accumulated wealth more than people and nature, the central issue is dehumanization from both inner and outer dimensions. When people self-determine or are told implicitly or explicitly that they are less valuable than another because they have less money, then they have to live with a view of self that is distorted by the assumptions behind it and that tends to devalue the gifts and capacities each individual brings into the world. This is the sacrifice we seem to be making at the altar of wealth as defined within the mainstream materialist paradigm.

How might transformation to a people-centric and land-based economy be fostered? We can really only affect that over which we have control. No matter the historical or cultural narrative told or digested, imposed or inherited, each of us is the author of our own experience. The turning point for transformation is in this reflection. From a moral standpoint, each of us has the capacity to give ourselves back to ourselves or reclaim ourselves from those who have co-opted that authorship. Yet, the inner path of overcoming even internalized oppression can be challenging for anyone, though the condition of the oppression and how it manifests may be different in the extreme. If there is an ideal for liberation, it is the liberation of each person's inner voice. Guidance for each human being is to be found there—it is that inner voice that speaks to injustice, speaks to right action, and tells us whether we are safe. The spiritual crisis is that we have been numbed to and disconnected from our inner voices. That is where each person's freedom resides, and it is the place from which we can find each other again in our humanity.

Despite how laws and policy are written, we have a responsibility for right nonviolent action (or civil disobedience). Despite how extractive and destructive profit driven economic activity is, we have to demonstrate a capacity for brotherhood and sisterhood through meeting each others' economic needs, even if this means outside the dominant money system. In other words we have to birth a new way of being in the world with each other—our spirits need to remain free, our laws and agreements need to respond the voice of each individual, and our economy needs to rest on sufficiency by assuring that each person's basic material needs are met while nature is restored as a result of economic life.

In a spiritual crisis, each individual, organization, and community has to take responsibility for its own moral condition regardless of whether the circumstances were legitimately caused by someone or something else, or caused by one's own actions. In the world of spirit, as I experience it, destiny is a compilation of choices; each person chooses her or his own path and, then, bears responsibility for those choices. It cannot be any other way though we may be deeply conditioned to think otherwise. Undoing the conditioning is akin to diving into the source and experience of inner oppression.

From this foundation, a crisis of the spirit can be transformed in a way that everyone feels connected to themselves, each other, and the world. This is the very opposite of how things lie now, and this sense for connection is an unaddressed longing spoken in many ways and in many languages. I would not harm that to which I am connected; whereas, what is characterized and treated as other can be easily written off, castigated, or eradicated devoid of a feeling for violence to the self.

If you are running a competitive race you want to see increasing distance from those behind you. Your chances of winning increase with every inch of separation. If, on the other hand, you are trying to build a house together, appropriate skills contributed, close communication, and interdependent progress are critical. No one wins, and the house stands as testament to collaborative effort. The polarity here is defined on one end by the rule of the individual (or competitive team), and on the other the rule of collaborative intention. By extension, the ends of these approaches point to radically differing and seemingly irreconcilable worldviews—survival of the fittest, or sustainability of the whole. This tension is pretty alive in the world right now, and the reconciliatory conversation, while rumbling in the underground, is rarely to be had where broad-scale change can be enabled.

Those who feel suspended in or stuck with this unhealthy condition in their hearts (and I count myself among that group) need to speak out more about it—not out of judgment (though that may be the greatest barrier to dialogue) but rather out of compassion for the suffering of those left without and equally for the suffering of those who have accumulated so much. Neither all the wealth in the world, nor all the poverty in the world, is antidote to the loneliness or isolation of dehumanization—perhaps the cruelest of human conditions. The reality is that there are real people with longing for community behind the screens of wealth and poverty. I would propose that some of them, as I am, are seeking partners to heal themselves, spiritual and relational divisions, and the world. Compassion is the invitation to dialogue, sufficiency the earthly cry of coexistence. So, what if love were the substance of wealth?

Equilibrium

4

MOVING TO EQUILIBRIUM

Risk and Return in the Next economy

The tandem term risk–return represents a kind of received wisdom in the investment world. The hyphen highlights the assumption that with higher risk comes higher return and that the investor's interest stands at the top of the investment system hierarchy. Such a unilateral perspective has produced enormous investment wealth very efficiently for a limited number of people—after all, only a few can afford to take the risks that produce the highest returns. Those below that threshold have options ranging from insured savings accounts (very low risk with minimal returns) to the casino world of slots, lotteries, and scratchers (with odds far outweighing risk in the calculus). There are a number of vehicles that lie somewhere between these extremes, such as CDs and bonds, but the risk–return choices are limited by regulation.

The point of this framing is not to cast aspersions on investors and the structures that support them in their deployment of capital, but rather to call into question the entwined nature of risk and return, coupled as they are in investor-centric practice, and to explore what might happen if they were treated as separate functions weighed out not only from the perspective of investor interest (private wealth) but also in light of community wealth. It is the rare exception in which this latter dimension is considered as anything other than a fortuitous byproduct of investment. The concept of the commonwealth holds little economic resonance in an individualistic ownership society. In an economy driven by competitive self-interest, what is not strictly economic suffers the most directly—namely, natural resources and culture, two key elements of the commons. I am pointing to a foundational problem with ownership. Do we own in order to accumulate wealth in service to self, or do we own in order to circulate and steward wealth in service to self *and others*? Each of these leading questions goes down a different path, and each to a world that has a fundamentally different economic operating system.

Historically, and from an economic perspective, the capacity to bring ideas into production has been the purview of the entrepreneur. The investor, able to recognize this capacity, places capital at the service of the entrepreneur who then uses those funds to run the business. Through the activities of the business an economic community is created including investors, employees, natural resources, suppliers, distributors, and customers, among others. Through its interconnected chain of actions this community produces wealth and hopefully the participants have their economic needs met from the proceeds of the ongoing circulation. However, through the assumed hierarchical power of the investor's position (high risk, high return) as it has come to be applied in the modern investing world, the natural flow of capital in economic community is driven to disequilibrium. Investment has moved from its original primary function as enabler of economic initiative, to a more extractive process, in that an investor's success has come to be measured by the degree to which wealth is drawn excessively out of community flow with far more than is necessary accumulated for private benefit. This is, of course, a broad-brush analysis. It is not intended as anti-capitalist or anti-anything, but rather to establish that the commonwealth could and should have a place in the investment process. Inclusion of the interest of the commonwealth could bring much needed equilibrium to the current extreme systemic imbalance, one caused at least in part by investor self-interest, and in the worst cases by greed.

The example of Mondragon Cooperative Corporation is a useful one for demonstrating that an investment system can create both personal wealth and commonwealth through a different set of assumptions about the risk–return linkage. The approach taken by Mondragon's financial institution, *Caja Laboral*, for investment is that a start-up enterprise is financed at a very low interest rate. This is so because the bank recognizes that a young business is not really in a position to carry a burdensome debt service. When the enterprise is established and can demonstrate sustainability, it then pays higher interest. This formula is quite the opposite of high risk, high return. Judging by Mondragon's growth and stability since the 1950s, it is worth understanding what lies behind this approach.

First, the consideration of risk is inherently broader than just the bank's perspective, because the bank is in reality owned by the community. Thus the failure of the enterprise is also the community's failure. This is not a conundrum, but instead a picture of financial and economic mutuality or interdependence that has long vanished from mainstream financial institutions, but has been the backbone of community banks and credit unions. Instead of the convention that risk is an indicator of what I as an investor might lose, risk is seen as a degree of investor and community commitment to a project's success. The rate of return is not at all derived from the perceived risk, but rather from what is needed in order for the money to continue in circulation and produce enough surplus to meet the complex of community needs. Much more could be said about the shared community values and agreements underlying Mondragon's system, but this is enough to see that Mondragon is one notable model of a different way of working.

There is change afoot. The emerging field of impact investing, which is looking at the outcomes of investing on the natural and cultural environment is moving toward a more bilateral view, one that recognizes the importance of the commonwealth and values it as a beneficiary. Yet, it fails to give that commonwealth a real voice in the investment process. The Global Impact Investing Network (GIIN) is one example, though it is still driven by the investor's will as the provider. The evolution of the B-corporation is another growing exemplar of reallocating investor–stockholder power to entrepreneurs who build a sense of the commonwealth into the corporate charter. In a B-corporation a risk to the environment caused by the company's activities is also a risk to the investor. Such an investor is not only stepping into a new set of agreements about stockholder rights, but also into an evolving social contract.

The realities of mutuality or interdependence are critical to maintaining economic equilibrium. And, further, owning with a sense of stewardship for the commonwealth will require a rewiring of most of our basic economic and financial understandings. In this case I have identified risk–return as a metaphoric magnifying glass to look into the system, which Occupy Wall Street (OWS) and so many others have named as broken, unjust, and even criminal. These visionaries for a new social contract have rightly identified that our current imbalance of wealth, and the concentration of economic power in the hands of investors, including Wall St. and banks, is the place where leverage for change is most needed and is most likely to be effective. One need not look far or read extensively to know that our economy is where the social pain is most visible and visceral.

Transforming from a culture of owning to a culture of stewarding will require a fundamental shift in how we view our relationship to the material world. If the last few years have taught us anything, it is that what we think of as material and enduring is no longer so. What we thought of as retirement savings can disappear overnight, and increasingly strong natural catastrophes can wipe out whole communities instantly. Communities rise up as the antidote to uncertainty, whether its origins are natural or cultural. OWS is nothing if not a new kind of community. While its origins reside in recognizing the disequilibrium in the economy, what the movement is demonstrating is a new stewardship of the commonwealth.

Portal

5

FAITH, HOPE, AND LOVE

Elements of an Appreciative Economy

I said to my soul, be still, and wait without hope.
For hope would be hope for the wrong thing; wait without love
For love would be love of the wrong thing; there is yet faith
But faith and the love and the hope are all in the waiting.
Wait without thought, for you are not ready for thought:
So the darkness shall be the light, and the stillness the dancing.

—T. S. ELIOT, *Four Quartets*

My economic behavior is governed by many things—mine and others' needs, desires, available resources and products, social value, and moral and ethical currents, to name a few. Much depends upon my presence of mind, how much I can slow my inner processes down to evaluate the circumstances, my strength to assess the source of desire, resist where I should, and then understand the reality of how one pays for the transaction, whether credit, cash, or other means of exchange. Imagine, if you will, all these transactions happening in an appreciative economy, one that values the warmth of recognition, inspiration, and relationships, supported rather than driven by economic activity. In an appreciative economy, money makes compassion more economically feasible than greed.

Financial transactions constitute a subset of broader economic activity. They are elements in the landscape of exchange. They have their qualities that I will explore from the perspectives of faith, hope, and love—not terms we normally associate with money. In the passage from *Four Quartets*, T.S. Eliot situates these concept–percepts in the soul as part of an inner dialogue: "I said to my soul...." They are connected to each other, yet each has its own characteristic gesture. I am motivated to engage in financial transactions for many of the reasons indicated. But, not all financial transactions are the same. For example, the same dollar can be used for a purchase, a loan, or a gift. Each use or function is distinguished by the degree of attention I pay to relationship and time. Just as the soul gestures of faith, hope, and love are distinct from each other, so, too, are the archetypal qualities of those transactions. But the two are connected as I experience them. By understanding how those qualities and their soul gestures are active in financial transactions, it is my hope to offer some inner reflective tools for bringing more consciousness to money and its uses toward an evolving appreciative economy.

FAITH

What do I mean by faith? The word denotes religious practices, but I would like to frame it from the perspective of a quality of soul. What is behind faith? And, how is it constructed such that I can recognize its presence regardless of a specific outer form or expression? First, my assessment is that faith, if not simply presumed by tradition, is built upon a complex of outer and inner inquiries and experiences over time. One superficial example is how one develops faith in a brand product. The first encounter is with the product and what the manufacturer and advertisers "promise" about how it will perform. That message is then either confirmed or contradicted by my experience with the product. Over time, I no longer have to evaluate whether or not I want to buy the product. If experience continually confirms the promise, the product has earned my loyalty and thus my faith in its value. The selection of that particular product is now part of my habit life, and of course makes my shopping time more efficient.

The point is that faith develops over time. It has an inherent historical framework, and usually a point of reference such as a body of religious knowledge or a consumer need. These kinds of faith are quite different in their degree of depth and the power they hold. Brand allegiance is not all that deep, or there would not be so much money spent on maintaining it. By contrast, imagine casually suggesting to someone that he or she change religion. Religion has a body of knowledge, values, and practices that have such cultural and historical reach that some are considered borne by blood. This could be considered a form of cell or tissue memory, a kind of atavistic presence that reaches well into the past.

Loan transactions share something of this historical aspect in the sense that I take a loan to accomplish something, purchase a house, for example, and then pay for the use of those funds over time—whatever the agreement established at the time. While I am writing the monthly check in the present, the true reference is to the historical event. Hopefully, as part of the loan origination, there was a great deal of due diligence done by both parties to the transaction. I want to know who is lending me the money, what the exact terms of the agreement are, and what the remedies are should they be needed. And the lender is likely asking me about my creditworthiness, my financial history, where I work and how much I make, etc. The purpose of this "dance" is to validate the history and intentions of the borrower (what I will do with the money), and to determine, based on that historical picture, whether or not the future will be consistent enough with that history in order to assure the success of the loan. In other words, does the lender have faith enough in me and the activity I want to finance to make the loan? And, do I as a borrower have enough faith in my ability to honor my loan commitment?

Loan transactions are based in faith, regardless of how objective the loan process may appear.

HOPE

When I say that I hope for something—someone's good health, or for something to happen—I am projecting an intention out into the future. Hope is future bearing. To attach specific outcomes or a time frame to it changes it from hope into an expectation. And, I have a different relationship to each, though I am not always clear in conveying which one I am actually inwardly holding. Pure hope is nothing but an open ended imagination that may inspire me or others, but leaves me or others free to act upon that hope or not. After all it is my hope, not theirs. This inner freedom is not of the political sort; it has nothing to do with rights or agreements. Instead, it arises from a spiritual, moral, or ethical place that only I can access or know for myself. Therefore, if I listen to my own hope and decide to realize it through my own volition, I have made a commitment or agreement with myself. It moves from hope to a kind of duty. If others respond to my stated hope, they also enter this same process for themselves. Although it may be quite gratifying for me, I also have to acknowledge that I have no control over the process of other individuals. They have taken it up out of their own inner freedom and for their own reasons.

Thus, hope has a deeply philanthropic aspect to it. When I make a financial gift, say to a charity, it only becomes a gift because I have given up any control of the money. If the gift comes with expectations or restrictions, it is still gift but not a truly free one. The standard acknowledgment line, which states that you have received no goods or services in return for the gift, is a simple expression of this deeper principle. One might say that a gift has a spiritual value in reciprocity for the sacrifice of any material value. (Tax benefits aside!)

The aspect of freedom is paramount for a gift. If I make a gift based on an intention and in freedom, and it is received in freedom and with recognition of that intention, then something quite new has happened in the realm of transactions—a kind of destiny moment in which two parties are aligned, and totally out of free choice.

And, the true gift aspect of a gift tends to operate outside the rational basis of time. When I make a gift to a charity, that gift is usually quickly transformed into purchase by the charity—to pay salaries, rent, buy equipment, or whatever. However, the gift element remains in the capacity of the charity to benefit lives. This aspect cannot be predicted. In educating a child, one does not know what capacity that individual will bring to the world, or when it may emerge. However, it is pretty likely that the educational process itself can be credited with having contributed to building that capacity. So a gift is entirely future bearing.

Gift transactions are based in hope regardless of the level of negotiation and agreement it might take to secure the gift.

LOVE

Love is so central to my well being, so critical to the buoyancy of my life, that its presence is ever-present. And in a way that is just the point. Love and the practice of love are relatively meaningless except in the present. Love is the tool by which I fully engage in the world and know what is coming toward me from the world, sometimes long before I can make sense of that knowing in my head. The practice of love is also the generator of the energetic field that I have around me that unconsciously interacts and exchanges with others. Love is essentially connected with our being rather than our doing.

It is a capacity of feeling that helps us to be awake to and interested in others and their needs. Because it is so linked with my presence, I should not, in the ideal, need to summon it as a force from some shadowed depths. It is instead a matter of my being awake to it as it speaks through my decisions and actions.

Thus, when I am making purchases, exchanging money for goods or services, it is neither faith nor hope that is qualitatively present, but rather, love. Purchases have no historical or future reference. The value is solely in the equality of exchange at the time. As I know only too well when reselling anything, the value may be very different in the next exchange. As opposed to loans and gifts, purchases happen very quickly and often in isolation. If I were to slow any of them down, all the variables that made that transaction possible might come into view: the thinking that went into the creation of the product; the labor that went into its production; the market that made it available; the vendor actually selling it; then the need that I have; the work that went into earning the money to make the purchase; my values... and so on. Suddenly, the purchase exchange represents the whole of our interdependent economic life encapsulated in one moment. There are potential challenges in this process. Because as a typical consumer I am seeking a good deal, I would have to be blind to the consequences of cheap labor, externalized costs, and environmental damage that allowed the price to be so low. If I were to slow down some purchases, I might actually be awakened to the mistreatment of people and animals that made such an advantageous price possible. I would be confronted with the discrepancy between my espoused values and how I practice them. If I am really paying attention to my authentic voice that actually knows and practices out of love, I would have to reconsider the purchase and maybe not even make it. Love arises from taking a deep interest in the reality I create for myself, from the empathic attention I pay to the needs of others, and from my ability to actively forgive what might otherwise feel like an insult coming toward me.

As I use money to purchase material goods to meet my needs, I am being informed more or less consciously by a part of my constitution formed during my infancy, one might say preconsciously. By this statement, I mean that at birth we are fully dependent upon our mothers (or surrogates) for our nurturance and nutrition. The quality of feeling that was connected with that process on the parent's part—the joy, the stress—are experienced as an associated part of the nurturance and thus become an integral part of our economic self. On one hand this could seem absurd, on the other it might help us to understand why money and how we use it, especially in the realm of purchase, is such a mystery to us, why we do not like to talk about it, and why it brings up all sorts of issues, particularly around the concept of what is enough. What need is really being met as we purchase to meet our needs (or, dare I say it, wants)? And, we purchase with such frequency, that we are hard put to have the time to pay consciousness to the process.

The practice of love, in the deepest sense of its meaning, is one way to bring healing through the consummation of purchase transactions.

CLOSING

The primary purpose of this inquiry is to connect qualities of soul to the qualities of financial transactions. I am asking myself, and the reader, to take a deeper look at our economic life, to recognize that how we are with our transactions inwardly is just as important as how we conduct them outwardly. It is a step toward integrating espoused and practiced values through our finances, a step toward reawakening the sacredness of our economic life. In the passage from the *Four Quartets*, what T.S. Eliot is urging the audience to do is to set aside all assumptions, cultural conditioning, and expectations—whether about the future (hope), present (love), or past (faith)—and for each of us to live into what our soul has to tell us.

When the soul inquiry we carry is about money and financial trans-actions, our place in them and their place in us, we may very well be in the frontier of transformative exploration: "So the darkness shall be the light, and the stillness the dancing." The practice of faith, hope, and love in financial transactions will then also invite that kind of transformation in others—as they experience the expression of my inner values and are touched by their own.

6

FROM EXPECTATION TO AFFIRMATION

An Inquiry into Transparency and Trust

The concept of transparency seems to be at the forefront of every discussion about our economy of late, and the majority of those discussions presume that the reader or listener knows what transparency means. I confess to being bothered by such presumptions— thus, this inquiry into transparency. It is an abstract concept, but one essential to our relationships and economic life. I hope one outcome of this brief inquiry is a deepened understanding of what is often the root cause of the call for transparency, namely, mistrust. Further, that transparency, understood in its full implications, can transform mistrust into a new and conscious trust, an essential ingredient for healing our economy and opening us up to a positive imagination for the future.

Transparency and trust are inextricably linked in human affairs, though transparency is best understood as a means not an end; and, trust is not a thing but rather a desirable multifaceted (my assumption) state of being that guides our actions.

What does transparency mean then in the context of finances? Most of us experience transparency in simple physics terms as we gaze out our windows to see the world with varying degrees of clarity. If we are moved to clear the film away so that we have a fuller, less mediated view, we are pointing to a process based upon increased visibility. In finances, if you cannot perceive or track what is going on with the transactions and "the numbers," seeking disclosure through auditing would be the parallel to window cleaning. The purpose and outcome would be to trust what you see.

But there are questions about finances that reach deeper than visibility and delve into the realm of assumptions. This is where transparency is no longer solely about facts or appearances, but rather about the conceptual aspects that drive the numbers and transactions. This quality of transparency is about making the invisible, visible—not what or how much, but rather the why of transactions. Of course, formulating and exposing assumptions takes us into the realm of values and judgment, and more importantly into the realm of reciprocity. By this I mean that transparency is a two-way process. We look out the window, while the rest of world can equally look in at us. Digging into the assumptions behind financial transactions, our own values and assumptions arise quite naturally as expectations about what we absorb of and reflect upon the information. Once we are comfortable with the assumptions and the resultant numbers, another level of trust emerges, one not as much tied to visibility, as it is to a quality of reciprocity. After all, the numbers represent human economic activity, and we expect to be able to see into that activity through the transactional agreement or accounting of it. This is no small feat. What hopefully becomes apparent through the reciprocal exploration is an affirmation of assumed values and intentions—a moment of deeper trust. Without this affirmation, unresolved expectations can lead to a kind of quiet conflict common to, but often unaddressed, in financial considerations.

Transparency and trust take another leap when there is an affirmation of mutual intentions among all parties to the transaction. This commonality of intention represents the possibility of a third level of trust that reaches through reciprocity and beyond agreement to a sense of shared vision, or appreciation of a common purpose. This level of trust engages a kind of idealism and engenders all manner of economic initiative and innovation.

In a way, there are three forms of trust that accompany financial transactions: trust in matter, or the observable; trust in others, their truth or integrity; and trust in spirit, or common intention. While transparency may on some levels feel like a right, as it is primarily treated in our current political debate on economics, it is also a vehicle for reaching trust in the three realms of matter, relationships, and common destiny. Thus the practice of transparency in finance, with full respect for the rights of privacy and safety, is an essential tool for transforming our economic future.

7

INTIMATIONS OF A NEXT ECONOMIC STORY

Given the very real tragedy of our current economy, we need a new economic story that dispels faulty assumptions about growth, the environment and our natural resources, and transforms the antisocial power of self-interested behavior along with the extractive practice of over-accumulation.

The new economic story is rooted in the incontrovertible reality of interdependence—social, ecological, and spiritual. At the same time, the new story honors cultural freedom and equality in matters political. The story embraces the value of dynamic tensions inherent in this construction. The new economic story restores to money its original purpose, to be put at the service of people who can use it to serve others, and eliminates the use of money solely to make more money. An essential part of the story is money as differentiated transactional functions—purchase, loan, and gift. Each of these functions has its own qualities that support not only the continual circulation of money, but also its renewal. The story assumes that economic activity will generate surplus capital, some appropriate portion of which will be reinvested in entrepreneurial innovation and some significant portion will be returned as gift to regenerate culture.

The story is based upon an understanding that all economic activity is actually initiated by gift, just as each of our breathing lives is supported at the outset by the gift of nourishment. That fluid gift is transformed through human development into capacities for new ideas and recognition of the needs of others. This is a snapshot of how a healthy culture contributes to economic renewal. Lending helps implement those economic ideas and the money is quickened by the use of loan (or gift) proceeds for purchase.

So the story portrays economic self-renewal through the continual flow and transformation of money through transactions. Economic life is actually managed collaboratively or associatively by representatives of all the parties affected by it. Thus, in the new story everyone's basic needs are present, and through the circulation of money our interdependence becomes transparent and life affirming. It is fully integrated. It is not only possible but also necessary for our survival. This is the new economic story characterized—nothing more than an intimation. It will take tremendous will, steadfastness of purpose, and an endless supply of social tact and grace to bring about this transformation. But first it is important to understand the intentions of the story itself, so it can support coherent action and be told compellingly to others.

Digging more deeply into the current economic story surfaces lots of apparently disconnected pieces. The story is laden with an abundance of impenetrable shadow elements and sorely lacking in the brilliant light of the possible. The story the media tells includes, but is not limited to: free markets as the primary approach to the world's problems; the benefit of competition regardless of its consequences; and, the inevitability of inequity and the value of accumulated wealth. The more I hear the story the more fictional, even cynical, it appears as the evidence of its rampant and unethical self-interest accumulates. I also suspect I am not alone in suffering dissonance as I live within a storied system that appears to be crumbling, while working to support the emergence of a new one, or, at least, one that operates on a drastically revised set of principles.

To see this emergence as a transformation rather than replacement of the old presents a problem. Transformation assumes an interconnected inter-influential world in which the potential new forms must lie somewhere within the existing one. To see this potential requires acceptance of it all, even the shadows. However, the economic story I tell myself is neither one of good versus bad, nor of suspended judgment. It is instead one that transforms: *assumptions about* to *direct experience of*; *power over* to *responsibility with*; and, *self-interest* into *service to*.

Most of the stories I am told about economics are based upon the dynamic of polarities, the haves and have-nots, management and labor, supply and demand, red and blue. This model of dualistic thinking has a long history in Western culture, but it no longer serves if the nonmaterial world of thoughts, feelings, and intentions is to be taken seriously. To this day, we are still teaching that our world is constructed around managing polarities. Faucets run hot and cold; batteries have positive and negative poles; gender is defined as male or female. At a material level these dualities serve as nothing more than identifiers or locators. They really have very little to do with how we make meaning out of experience; instead, meaning emerges through the interaction of multiple polarities. When we sense temperature, or electric current, or the human psyche, we are looking at indicator concepts that acknowledge a field created through the co-presence and movement of polarities. For example, though I am male, I am aware of both masculine and feminine qualities that operate within my character and inform my interactions with the world.

If we are to have a new economic story, it will require a shift in thinking that sees money in the same light—as an indicator concept, an energetic field, which is not a thing or commodity but a circulating measure and store of value that itself arises from the relationship between unused resources and unmet needs in economic life. The essential point is: If we are to transform the current economic story to a new one, whether you agree with my telling of it or not, we are going to have to change our thinking to include the notion that every material matter has a nonmaterial counterpart; and, further, that each of us stands as measure of the dynamic energy field that arises from their constant interactions. How we choose to act as economic beings, individually or collaboratively, can transform the economic story, and at the same time, bring positive change to culture and the processes of governance as a byproduct. Such is the power of story.

Uncertainty

8

THE CENTER IS UNCERTAIN

Further Notions of a Next Economic Story

Farmers have much to teach us about money and the economic climate. Good farmers now know that they can no longer count on historical weather patterns; instead, they speak of climate chaos and are challenged to farm with a new consciousness. Their planning has had to let go of past expectations, and instead they attend to deeply observing, anticipating, directly participating in, and reacting to the climate as an immediate phenomenon—changeable, unpredictable, filled with events of an unprecedented scale. For farmers, global warming is only one facet of the new *chaord,* a delicate and shifting condition that holds both chaos and order as co-present and a term coined by Dee Hock.

In a *New York Times* op-ed piece of November 28, 2010, "An Almanac of Extreme Weather," Jack Hedlin, a Minnesota farmer, explained the plight of farming in the era of climate change: "Climate change, I believe, may eventually pose an existential threat to my way of life. A family farm like ours may simply not be able to adjust quickly enough to such unendingly volatile weather. We cannot charge enough for crops in our good years to cover the losses in the ever-more-frequent bad ones." The production or market farmers I know, even the biodynamic ones, have been worried about this issue for more than a few years now. What Hedlin has touched on is not only symptomatic of agriculture but also has broad-reaching implications for all of how economic life sustains us, or not. So, uncertainty, whether you think of it as a concept or feel it as a condition of psyche, is central to and, to a degree, defines our lives and our times. It plays at the boundary between our desire to know and control, and the capability of functioning effectively in the ambiguity that characterizes the chaord.

There are many uncertainty parallels between agriculture and our financial system. The extreme financial "market" events of the last few years have devastated the economy, just as the volatile weather events have wiped out whole farm crops at short notice. The restoration process, whether rebuilding a retirement fund or the fertility of the topsoil, is long. What distinguishes the financial markets from agriculture is that while farmers are privileged to steward natural systems, financiers operate in a world that is entirely human-made. It is our own invention and thus has within it both the genius and flaws of human character.

That human nature could be considered disconnected from the rest of the natural world, or that humanity is the master of nature are both fictive concepts. From an economic standpoint, from the perspective of how we work in the world to meet each other's material needs, such fiction is used to justify how one person can benefit from another's sacrifice and how we can continue to consume and waste nature for the sake of undue profit. To accept the fictive concepts, and narrative that follows from them, means that the moral foundation, one might even say purpose, of our economic interdependence is debased. This is one way to make sense of, but not explain away, the abysmal Wall Street actions in which bets were made against the best interests of people, whether in securities (an ironic name), derivatives, or hedges, in the name of profitability. A culture without a moral compass is also a chaord because it is so vulnerable to the whims or intentions, good and bad, of individual action with no force of accountability or law. This is not to condemn all financial markets, just as I would not condemn all agricultural practices. It is a question of whether those practices contribute to healing or further destroying nature and the integrity of human nature.

Farmers and investors who have chosen or are choosing a healing path are developing new approaches and new capacities to operate with integrity in functional uncertainty. Some investors now know that modern portfolio theory no longer works; its assumptions, based on certainty of patterns, are in serious question. This theory, it turns out, assumed that the world operates with machine-like predictability, and that the theory itself would suffice as a predictor of market behavior and return. Does the risk–reward paradigm still make sense in light of how closely it has come to resemble gambling? Risk, it seems, is an index of possible failure. Actuarial methodology is devoted to understanding, measuring, and managing risk. It is all based on a gesture of protection and distrust, and consciously excludes uncertainty from its formulas. But it is uncertainty that most directly affects us.

What does investing look like if uncertainty is recognized as a central tenet? How does one develop trust that an entrepreneur or enterprise will be successful and over what time frame? One might say that a new approach to investing is like a farmer planting a crop. You prepare and plow the field as best as you can, pay full attention to all the natural forces at work, pay loving attention to the plants as they grow while in deep observation of the environment, weather, climate, prepared to make adjustments—sometimes it means frost protection at 4:00 in the morning. These are all part of an active engagement that places a premium on minute-by-minute human attention and a capacity for anticipation, always with a view of long-term outcomes. This kind of engagement leaves no room for a mechanistic view, no room for passive assumptions, and treats uncertainty as real and present, and as a prime motivator for bringing a healing impulse into the world.

Uncertainty has a role to play in our transforming consciousness. Uncertainty pushes the boundaries of knowing in a new way that may not fit within conventional science, since it assumes we are part of rather than master of world. This view means that we (human nature) suffer as the environment suffers, that everyone's future is equally uncertain despite the inequity of resources. We are fully interdependent; and our inner climate inseparable from the outer. So, the balancing force to uncertainty resides in how we work with others in and through our social structures: of relationship, community, and work; how we develop trust, create our agreements, and engage out of natural interest in each other. This is also an imagination of risk sharing as a new strategy for risk mitigation and management.

For anyone seeking a spiritual path, uncertainty is a call to practice. With this call in mind, due diligence takes on a new level of discipline, one that adds imagination and intuition to the analysis. The marketplace as it currently exists places great emphasis on results and commodities, with little interest in the consequences for human sustainability and soil fertility. The investor and the farmer will find this set of priorities transformed when they recognize that they do not really decide or operate solely for themselves out of self-interest, but rather are long-term contributors to the broader value-creating community, whether local, regional, or global.

When uncertain events occur, community is the first responder because the value of the activity, farm, or enterprise is held as essential to the sustainability of the community itself. Thus, understanding community, imagining it, testing it, setting prices with it are part of a new discipline that will inevitably change the financial system. Uncertainty can be a powerful teacher as we invite it in from the shadowy margins of our financial systems. As we learn to live with and celebrate its ambiguity, we will likely be more awake to discerning those opportunities that recognize economic interdependence, and those investments that bear the seeds of a more social and livable economy. Such a change will also require a reframing of outcomes and purposes. The outcome of farming: soil fertility with commodity production a byproduct. The outcome of investment: economic renewal and equilibrium with return as a byproduct. Living into uncertainty can certainly bring about the needed shift in our priorities for a next economy.

WORK

9

AN EVOCATIVE ETHOS

Making a Living in the Next Economy

In the ideal of the next economy, there would be no distinction between work and vocation. For example, because writing now requires so little physical effort, so little friction, I can more easily voice my thoughts through the invocation of language and text. So, I am practicing my vocation—not only what I am called to do, but also what I call out publicly as matters for community consideration.

In our current economy, vocation, what one is called to do, is one thing, making a living is often another. There is instructive history behind this disintegration. We know that the Industrial Revolution made the specialization and productive efficiency of the division of labor a permanent fixture of the economic landscape. Skip back further to the 17th century, and consider the implications of French philosopher René Descartes's mind–body dichotomy. In economic terms, this dichotomy became a basis for a different "division of labor"; that is, a division between people's physical labor and their capacity to think—a dehumanizing process that served capitalism well and culture poorly. To a degree the mind–body problem still informs the present. With this as background, I am proposing that in the next economy, the ethic of work means a remerging of labor and thinking, of making one's living and living one's vocation. For a vocation to constitute a living entails a job with income, compels a degree of self-development to keep the job meaningful, and requires engagement in a work community that encourages new ideas and practices.

I also know how far we are from this ideal as I describe it, given the current state of economic affairs. The number of people who would be relieved just to have a job for which they are paid, even better a living wage, is unconscionable. Job creation, meaningful work, is a priority, not just for the economy, but also for the value it contributes to each person's overall well being. Speaking of such an ideal of work while so many suffer is a risk and smacks of privilege. However, my purpose is certainly not to belittle or insult anyone, or to appear arrogant. Instead I want to posit an imagination of work that challenges the current (old) paradigm and system that: casts labor as a commodity; people as replaceable, to be used up for the sake of profit generation; and, sees the funding of culture, which supports the enrichment and renewal of people, as an annoying and unnecessary expense. My purpose is also to put forward an imagination of work that serves what is deeply human, prioritizes people over things, and recognizes sufficiency and interdependence as determinants in balancing individual and global needs. From the perspective at ground level, the evidence indicates that not much connected to the old, but still dominant, paradigm is working very well right now—except for those at the top of the financial heap.

So what does the imagination of work in the next economy look like? I would like to take the radical position that by reclaiming some historical understandings of work and vocation, I can evidence a more humanized and humanizing view of economic productivity than that practiced in the modern industrial model.

Daily life in a Benedictine Monastery is broken into a three-part rhythm. The segments are called *ora*, *labora*, and *lectio* (prayer, work, and study)—three hours of prayer and meditation, five hours of labor, and two hours of study. Prayer, of course, is the work of monastics, but they also have to eat and have clothing and shelter; in short, they also have a practical economic life. In the *lectio* they have something of what we would call a learning community, in which they serve one anothers' development through shared experience of Biblical text and reading commentaries. Of course, the "output" of the monastery is spiritual, or religious, in nature, so one could dismiss its somewhat island-like quality as irrelevant to modern commercial culture. But monasteries have lasted a long time and support the people who dwell in them, while bringing about significant, though not always positive, cultural change through service to community.

A second, and current, example of a different view of work in economic life can be found in the Sarvodaya village movement in Sri Lanka, founded by A.T. Ariyaratne. In the villages, they do not speak of full employment. That is essentially a Western industrial concept (rarely accomplished). Instead they speak of full engagement. What does that mean exactly? First one has to understand the Buddhist economic concept of right livelihood—that is to say that each and every person in a community, regardless of age or condition, has the capacity to contribute to the overall economy and cultural life of the community, and in return can have one's basic needs met out of the work of the community. One example: Roads are built by the community. If all one can do for the day, given the limitations, is to move one stone into place in the roadway, it is honored and considered as that person's contribution. In the Sarvodaya framework, economic activity is not separate from the spiritual or political life, and right livelihood is a correlative of vocation. Still one could say that this approach only solves economic issues one village at a time, but the point here is the human quality and value of work.

There have been and are numerous examples of workplaces in which the recognition of people's need for a sense of growth, learning, or development has been met with some innovative activities. Early in the twentieth century Rudolf Steiner gave lectures for the workers of the Waldorf Astoria Cigarette factory as an antidote to the deadening effects of modern factory production. Such activities were deemed important by the management not because it would increase production or profit, but rather because the workers were people, each of whom had an inner life of mind or spirit as well as the physical capacity to labor. As another example, the development of team production in auto manufacturing takes into account a quality of participation and problem-solving that engages the workers on a deeper level than just repetitive physical labor.

But there is one element in this more humanized view of work that I have not seen addressed as we point to a next economy. And, until it is addressed all the new thinking about work and the new workplace will still be anchored in the old paradigm. That element is compensation. The way of life in the monastery or the Sarvodaya village is contained enough such that compensation is integral. You work in community, and your needs are met in community. This imagination offers much by way of a future picture, especially if our money economy collapses entirely. The reality is that all our needs are met in community whether we think of this on a local or global scale.

Though in common parlance we do not think of it this way, compensation speaks of the function of money as a replacement for what we cannot provide ourselves or that our community will not provide without compensation for its needs. If we do not have the time, capacity (or interest) to labor in the field for food, we need to compensate someone to do this on our behalf. But, what is money "buying"? The food—it would appear that way when we go to market. The labor to produce it—we certainly know there is a cost to production built into price. The old paradigm is predicated on labor itself as a commodity, something that can be bought and sold, and priced on an hourly or annual market rate. Such an approach will always tie work to a direct line between input and output of money or capital, and thus to a division of labor and efficiency—no matter how nice the workplace or the benefits.

Vocation, however, does not operate on such a linear path because it assumes a flow between spirit (calling) and work (how that calling translates into the world). And we know that vocation is highly individualized. The lesson to be taken from the village and the monastery is that right livelihood needs to be supported, and when that is done a sufficient and sustaining economy emerges. The work one does is part of one's life path, one's gift to community, not a thing separate or separable from the one who does it. Compensation, then, is not payment for work, but rather payment to free one to work—out of vocation or capacity and on behalf of others. This logic indicates that compensation should be paid in advance of the work so that personal material needs (housing, food, etc) are met and the work can be freed to focus on its benefit to community. This shift would create a new ethos of work, one that disconnects compensation from performance, and one that continues to invite the integration of one's vocation and work as inspiration for a more ethical and humanized economy.

Heraldic Emblem

10

ON COMPENSATION,
OR WHAT AM I WORKING FOR?

No question, how and what we get paid is something we take personally. So, understanding compensation is difficult from philosophical and emotional standpoints. The issue comes with layers of complexity—the stories we tell ourselves about self-worth and a host of other conditioned assumptions about our value, the marketplace, and the organizations in which we work. This should come as no surprise, because the experiences and associations we carry are often framed in a materialist paradigm constantly reiterated in the mainstream business world and through the media. As a typical example, an advertisement in a recent *New York Times* read: "Earn what you're really worth." This is the kind of reductive message that reinforces the notion that "I am what I earn" and nothing more. The materialistic paradigm embraces the story of compensation as an extension of self-interest. Other aspects of one's being, like our moral character, our capacities, and our need for love are essentially dismissed as subjective or "soft" indicators, even though these are what actually guide my relationships, what I care about, and my ability to discern meaning in life.

For organizations, compensation is a conscious or unconscious, and often inconsistent expression of organizational behaviors, its culture, the predilections of its decision makers, the organization's history and habits, and its practiced values. One could say that each paycheck marks the intersection of two systems, personal and organizational. And since organizations are also social in nature, there are additional layers of assumptions, judgments, appreciations, and aspirations about compensation permeating social systems that remain unaddressed. Under the conditions described here, compensation is basically antisocial and furthers self-interested behavior patterns.

If we are striving to build organizations of people working to lead a regenerative future-bearing economy, however, it is hard to imagine how any organizational coherence, transparency, and mutual understanding of compensation could be achieved without a philosophical covenant based on organizational purpose, values, and principles. And further that this covenant is cultivated and shared by the people working together in that organization. Included in this transformative imagination is first a reconsideration of the nature of work and secondly the relationship of compensation to it—in essence our livelihood.

We can readily grasp how compensation is tied to labor if we assume it is a commodity. Most of us have been raised with this assumption embedded in our psyche, our payroll systems, and in law. I get paid an amount for an hour's work. If an organization or individual is willing to pay, I can charge more for it. Its perceived value goes up, even though I am the same person regardless of the price. The fact is that whatever I can charge has nothing to do with me as a human being. Rather, this is how market forces work in the world of commodities. In the capital system, producers are constantly trying to reduce the cost of labor in search of higher profit margins. Labor in this sense is a disposable commodity to be replaced with a cheaper version, as profit matters more than the quality of life of the person who is producing that profit. In this system, individuality is sacrificed for the sake of efficient markets—that is to say profitability and return on investment.

The laws of commodities are different than the laws of being human. Things, commodities, the products of human labor, are naturally part of the circulation of goods and services, and are subject to economic forces that have no rightful relationship to the real value of a human being. The market operates on the assumption that an employee is nothing more than his or her labor, and any two or a thousand people are all equal in this regard, that is to say uniformly treated as commodities. If we are really trying to understand how compensation works on a human level, ponder the following: Why does a professional baseball player make a million dollars to play a game, while a teacher makes considerably less, even though students' futures are critically dependent upon the quality of that teacher's work? What does this tell us about compensation, and what does it tell us about the relationship between what we vitally value and how that value shows up in the world of money?

We are unlikely to make any progress through our current state of extreme resource inequality, or achieve any level of economic sufficiency, until we realize that labor is not a commodity. The drive to reduce the cost of labor, and to treat it as a commodity to be bought and sold, displaced and replaced, is derived from the competition to maximize profit. This extractive approach has left much human and environmental degradation behind.

In 1914, the Congress of the United States declared in its Clayton Act: "The labor of a human being is not a commodity or article of commerce." This was done in part as a protection against abuse of labor around which the labor union movement had been formed. Thirty years later the same notion, that labor is not a commodity, was reiterated as part of the International Labor Organization's *Declaration of Philadelphia* (10 May 1944). In a way, both statements settle the labor as commodity question by saying what it is not. Yet, neither offers an affirmative insight into labor in such a way that the sense and purpose of compensation are on clear ground.

If labor is not a commodity, then what is it? And what then is the purpose of compensation?

Labor is a resource in the same way that nature is a resource. Each human being has the capacity to tap that resource to work in the physical world and further to turn that capacity in service to the interdependent realm of economic activity. One could say that labor is pre-economic. In the sense that buying and selling are economic, it makes sense to say that you cannot buy labor, but rather the product of that labor.

Then one has to ask, what is this resource of labor? Where does it come from? I do not know any other way to answer that question than to call it gift, a gift that is part of the essential nature of a human being to be developed though life and practical activities. To be a gift, it cannot be bought. Rather, it has to be received as such and then transformed to be of service. While labor is a resource within each person, no two individuals manifest that resource in the same way. Capacities are different; circumstances are different. This is at the core of understanding individuality.

Individuality, the uniqueness of each human being, stands in stark contrast to the homogenizing standard of value that we call money. This standardization is both inherent in the function of money and necessary for the flow of economic activity. The result is that compensation is a holder of both/and. No wonder the tension and complexity. Compensation serves to support and free an individual to bring her or his gifts and capacities in service to others through production, and when received to enable that individual to participate in the rest of economic life through expending the money. There is a kind reciprocal poetic to this process if one imagines that an individual receives a gift of labor as resource, puts that gift in service to an organization (or to one's own enterprise) with the result that compensation flows back as a result of the organization's collective activity, and then again disperses and disappears back into the economy as individuals each use their respective compensation to meet material needs.

I hope I have painted a picture of a participatory economy, one that recognizes the value of each human being, not as a commodity but as a necessary resource and co-creator. Further, compensation has a very particular role to play in this broader context. If you accept the assumptions and implications of the advertisement mentioned at the beginning—I should earn what I am really worth—then you have made yourself a commodity. Though one might successfully sell oneself, there is a price to pay. But what is that price? What is the sacrifice? I would say that to commoditize oneself, or to commoditize others by putting a price on them is a measure of dehumanization. This is the very opposite of the direction we need to go in order to create a regenerative economy. I would rather reframe compensation as liberating human capacity in order that each may be of service and contribute to an interdependent world.

ORGANIZATIONS

11

CLOSING THE CREDIBILITY GAP

The Value of Nonprofit Governance

Governance is a social process. Its history is as long as that of societies, which organized themselves by creating a set of operating agreements, oral or written. This history is part of us, our collective inheritance and carried by us at the cellular level. Consciously or unconsciously, it lives in how we form our life as individuals and as social beings; it manifests in the multitude of agreements that make daily life manageable. Grammar governs language; the colors of traffic signals govern traffic safety. The United States Constitution is a body of evolving agreements, which frame our rights. Government, or the political state, grew out of governance processes as human consciousness evolved from organizing around hieratic or theological order to the more demotic and secular forms of modern day. This evolutionary development and the ongoing dynamic between the rule of "church and state" reflect the evolution of our consciousness as social beings whose needs are both material and spiritual. We recognize the need for governance in the material world, but bridle at governance of matters spiritual. Yet we are bound to work together out of the gifts of our individualities. That is the modern condition and a rising dilemma since the quality of governance, which we have inherited, comes primarily from ancient Rome. The Romans were masters of the material world. They developed law in the form that we know it—the powerful few

creating agreements for the many—and practiced governance impe-
rially, controlling, and centrally directed. In essence, in the Roman
Empire, power meant power *over*.

Lost in this narrative from Western history are forms of governance that could be characterized in the lineage of community
self-determination and that were based upon circles, collaboration,
trust, equality, and, ideally, altruism—in essence power *with*. In
this context, agreements are more consensual. Yet, this latter picture is not what comes to mind when one mentions the word governance in most organizational settings. Instead it conjures a force
outside ourselves that, at best, protects our rights, and at worst,
attempts to control our thoughts. Thus we have a natural tendency
to see individual freedom and governance in terms of duality or
polarity, or, in the extreme, in terms of conflicting forces. Now is
the age of questioning authority. And, why not, when a governing
body can be held responsible for creating a "credibility gap," a
phrase coined in 1963 to name the misalignment between known
facts about the Vietnamese War, and the story that was being told
by governmental agencies for self-serving purposes. Forty-five
years later the phrase seems prophetic.

It is time for the redemption of governance. It is time to
restore it to its rightful function in service to the positive ends of
credibility, trust, transparency, and freeing up of human capacity. And, I believe that the nonprofit, independent sector has the
capacity and responsibility to lead this way because nonprofits
are governed by volunteers—and thus out of spiritual rather than
material motivation, out of love for mission and through the gifting of time. In speaking to the supposed polarity between individual freedom and a body of laws or agreements, Albert Sch-
weitzer wrote the following in *Christianity and the Religions of
the World*: "As modern men we imagine the state of the perfect
human society to be one of harmony between legal organization
and the practice of love.

Jesus does not attempt to harmonize justice and love but says to us: If you want to be in the spirit of God, you may not think or act otherwise than in love." Although this is coming from a particular religious viewpoint, it holds much wisdom for the future of governance practice by establishing love, and the trust that attends it, as the ultimate value. In some ways it might be possible to imagine that if we lived in pure love and trust, we would need no governance structures at all. Instead we would recognize and be guided by the highest of altruistic or spiritual principles in community and global life—principles living so deeply in our hearts that we would need no written code except the meeting of human beings— but this is a picture for the future.

ORIGINS OF GOVERNANCE IN HUMAN DEVELOPMENT

Governance is not a thing outside of us. It is a faculty we exercise inwardly for ourselves constantly as we live our lives. Understanding how we come to govern ourselves, that is, how we develop this inner capacity from birth to adulthood has much to offer toward renewing our imagination and practice of good governance in organizations. For the sake of transparency I would like to say that this notion occurred to me during a presentation on child development given by a wise and experienced educator. Her insights were based upon years of observation of children and an extraordinary understanding of Rudolf Steiner's insights into human development. My addition is the translation of these thoughts into terms of governance with the hope of transforming assumptions about power into a framework of empowerment. I beg your patience as I try my best to articulate these concepts.

The period from birth to approximately seven years old is the time when we learn primarily through movement and play to support the developing senses. Early childhood specialists also note that young children learn through imitation. But there is another aspect when observing this phase of development. Newborn babies are one hundred percent dependent upon caring parents or other adults to have their physical needs met. Babies are thus first and foremost economic citizens and the degree to which caring adults demonstrate care, they also demonstrate, or model, accountability for the natural trust necessarily accorded to them. Therefore, although children learn through imitation, they are at the same time taking in pictures of accountability, as demonstrated the parents, on a cellular level.

From seven to fourteen years old, the central theme in development is the capacity for authority through the teacher modeling authority. This is done, for example, through appropriate discipline in the earlier part of this seven-year cycle, which the children then internalize and transform into self-discipline. From another perspective, in the first and second grade teachers will author stories and other material that the children copy. Over time, authorship for material is taken up by the children as they each evolve toward increasingly more generative stages, and thus become authors. This is preparation for each child's later recognition that she or he is actually author of and has authority for her or his own experience and life.

In the third cycle, from fourteen to twenty-one, the key theme is that of responsibility. During this time one learns about one's own personal strengths and gifts and begins to explore the rightful task or profession in life. By the quality and depth of intellectual inquiry, the inspiration of teachers and other adults, and real life experience, one learns how to be responsible for oneself, others, and the world. The culmination of this cycle occurs at about twenty-one. At this time the ego or "I," which has been slowly and steadily forming and maturing through the early years comes to the foreground. Its emergence is signaled by a growing awareness of identity and self in relation to the world. This ego now has a new capacity to manage the functions of accountability, authority, and responsibility, developed along the way and to reflect on them as part of integrity and working effectively in and for the world. This combined visionary and reflective capacity is the ability to govern oneself, to have a sense of purpose and meaning in life, and to make decisions large and small in the context of a destiny path and the agreements one makes with oneself.

I think it is important to realize that nonprofit organizations have destiny paths and operate within a framework of agreements. And yet the "ego" can take two paths. One path is the directive path that flows from a singular source and controls the actions and participants in the organization. The other is the collaborative path in which the "ego" resides in the agreements between the participants and frames the limitations of the actions, though it may have a singular manager. This latter is to my mind the way of the future, but it is entirely dependent upon a very highly evolved capacity to develop, abide by, and hold each other accountable to agreements—in love and trust.

Early in the twentieth century, Rudolf Steiner, founder of Anthroposophy, formulated a social philosophy that identifies three cooperative sectors of social life—economic, rights, and spiritual–cultural. He recognized in each sector a qualitative principle that could guide understanding of the human values at work in them. They are: interdependence in economics, equality in rights, and freedom in the spiritual–cultural realm. This profound view serves as background and inspiration for my views on governance.

GOVERNANCE FRAMEWORK AND TRUSTEESHIP

Authority, what attaches to it and what flows from it, may be one of the great inner questions and organizational struggles of our time. In the cultural context of our cherished individual freedom, we are our own authority. We work hard to protect that authority and react strongly when others interfere with it. Within this context, I decide who decides, even when I give that authority over to another—who hopefully receives it on my behalf.

And yet, we all live together. We do so within a framework of agreements micro and macro, some unconscious, some conscious, some constitutional, some convenient, some in constant creation. There is one consistent aspect of meaningful and constructive agreements, however: No agreement can be created unilaterally for another party. What begins as freedom for the individual is transposed at that moment into the freedom to create an agreement between two equal parties. This engenders the following questions: How might an organization create a system of agreements that can recognize the authority of the individual and the equality of each in relationship within the system of mutual agreements? How might an organization agree to enforce those agreements in a consequential system of accountability? These questions are contained in a larger one concerned with governance.

Framed in another way, one could say that the constructive purpose of governance is to lay the ground rules for leadership, authority, responsibility, and accountability within an organization, and to advance the purpose for which that organization was created in the first place. Governance is a function not an end. In a for-profit corporate structure, it is very clear that the shareholders are owners and hold the primary authority for the entity, though there are currently innovations in corporate structures that are emphasizing the rights of the public as an integral part of corporate code. However, nonprofit, IRS Section 501(c)(3) charitable organizations have no stockholders as owners. Instead the trustees are charged with making sure that the interests of the public are met through the mission of the organization. Just as a corporation, for better or worse, has the rights of an individual with the interests of the stockholders paramount, the ultimate authority for who decides who decides in a nonprofit resides with the trustees. These principles of authority are relevant to all self-administered or self-governed public benefit organizations. I would like to add that these principles are essential to maintaining independence from direct government interference in the organization. In all cases, the laws of the land are fundamental and nonnegotiable.

All authority for a not-for-profit corporation resides in the incorporating trustees of the corporation. This group, as a group, is granted its authority by the state, which charges it with fulfilling a charitable or educational mission. Given this fact, which has legal, social, and spiritual implications for the organization, it follows logically that the board of trustees holds and originates all delegation of authority within the boundary of the mission. The trustees are thus responsible for determining the conditions and limitations of that delegation.

The corporation, the primary legal or "physical" body of the school, is entrusted to the Board of Trustees, which serves the public by standing in, so to speak, for the broader "ownership" or "community" of the organization. This public aspect of the nonprofit is often further defined by who the organization intends to serve, by the articles of incorporation, the bylaws, the mission statement, and even the IRS 990 tax form filed annually. From a governance and economic perspective this aspect of the corporation has a character unto itself that is different than but includes the day-to-day life of organization. Understanding this distinction is central and critical to understanding good governance. Essentially there are two entities, or an organization within a community. The board governs corporation, the legal organization, while the organization serves its community or constituency.

The community consists of all the clients served as well as any others who are drawn to this community through shared values, services, or practices on a conscious or unconscious level. The staff and trustees of the nonprofit, in addition to their respective governing or operational responsibilities, are also members of this community and are really there as equal participants in its life. Thus, the members or leaders of the nonprofit are a part of the cultural aspects of the organization's work as well as carrying its corporate functions.

As a self-governed, self-administered nonprofit, that part of the entity devoted to creating and providing the program comes into being within the corporation. From another perspective, the program operates under the aegis of the corporation. In either case, it is important to note that the corporation and the program or programs are not the same forms, though of course neither would exist without the other. Interestingly enough, clients and members of the nonprofit are connected to the corporation by association membership, dues, or fees (economics), and to the program (cultural) through its public benefit service.

Given this background, governance, leadership, and initiative—all important elements of a healthy and active organization—need a framework of agreements and appropriate communication forms that reflect and serve the mission, and make clear the terms of how individuals, committees, and the public at large are knit together in furthering that social mission.

DELEGATION, DAY-TO-DAY MANAGEMENT, AND THE INTERSECTION OF TWO ENTITIES

Authority, responsibility, and accountability are the three integral legs of good governance and should never be separated. If one is going to delegate one of the three, the other two are necessarily delegated as part of the package. To do otherwise makes governance ineffective. When governance is ineffective, decision-making is compromised and the organization suffers. There is a threefold picture here. Authority emerges in the sphere of rights and agreements. Responsibility arises from the sphere of individual gifts and capacities (cultural/spiritual). Accountability attends to the sphere of economics, the sphere of meeting needs. In the name of good governance, a Board of Trustees, which receives all the authority, responsibility, and accountability from the state at incorporation, needs to have a clear recipient to whom to delegate in order to manage day-to-day activities.

The delegation of authority in this context is one of the most misunderstood aspects of governance in nonprofits. Governance and management are different, but are often confused. The board is a group of volunteers who gather around the furtherance of a mission to ensure that the corporation fulfills its promise to the public. Its purpose is not to manage the organization, but to account to the public for the organization's performance. Since the board is not there every day (and should not need to be) they need someone(s) to whom they can delegate the authority, responsibility, and accountability (a,r,a). Where an executive director or other similar position is present, it often receives or arrogates that mandate or delegation. He or she then in turn is free to delegate (a,r,a) for any aspect of the program to another person or group. Thus, the executive function operates in the intersection between the corporation and the public community, between the trustees and the community. If there is truth to the adage that no one can serve two masters, then it is no wonder that leading an administration is such a challenging occupation.

If the volunteer board is to govern successfully and to explore and expand its connections to the wider community, it cannot spend its limited time on arguing over delegation, who has authority for what, or worried about whether the building is safe. They need to know that the quality of program, legal and financial matters, the stewarding of relationships, and organizational effectiveness are being managed. When that is not happening, those kinds of conversations drain everyone's energy, energy that could be much better spent building for the future. On the other hand, once the delegation is made and agreements clear, the board has to fully trust (based on good reporting procedures) that delegation and not act outside its realm by managing the day-to-day affairs.

THE LANDSCAPE OF ORGANIZATIONAL DISCIPLINE

Once governance is in place, and all agree to trust and abide by the delegations and policies, the threefold principles of freedom in the cultural or spiritual life, equality in rights and agreements, and interdependence in economics take on a new and dynamic quality. A well-governed organization is far more likely to maintain its cultural freedom the more deeply it understands and manages its realms of economics and rights agreements.

When an individual chooses to accept an offer of employment at a nonprofit, she or he has made that choice out of freedom. However, once accepted, she or he is also agreeing to abide by all of the existing policies and thus is no longer free in the same way, though she or he is always free to choose to leave the organization. This is what is meant within the concept of "at-will" employment. It is important to keep in mind that the policies are a living body of agreements, which can be changed through orderly process over time. Each member of the organization is free to request that an agreement be reconsidered. Most important, each person needs to be, and is, free to fulfill his or her responsibilities as best as possible within the framework of those agreements and delegations.

One of the practices of economic interdependence as indicated by Rudolf Steiner (here paraphrased) is: The degree to which I work to meet the needs of others, my needs will be met. As a reflection of this principle, the accountability structure in a nonprofit should recognize that each organ is a part of the whole, that the task of each group in accomplishing its work is to support the success of the others—interdependence. For example, success in the program and success in client relations support the success of the development staff. Each person's work affects the whole system and each person is affected by the system. Thus, the value of each person in the work community is recognized, with the result that there is no unintended (or intended) class hierarchy, for example, between staff and clients. There is just the exercise of different capacities for appropriate tasks.

The realm of agreements is one of equality, a democratic form, one person one vote. The trustees work in this way as they exercise the duties of care and loyalty. Sometimes there is confusion when staff members serve as voting trustees because they are not there to manage, but rather to govern and serve the higher needs of the organization—as are all trustees. For example, *if* there is distrust of or a lack of confidence in the board by the staff *and* there are three staff members serving as voting board members, *then* there are three trustees (those three staff members) living with internal conflict and divided loyalties. Staff members who serve as trustees are not "representing" the staff in their board work, but are trustees equal with all other trustees and share in the duties of care and loyalty practiced by the board as a whole. Board members are each expected to make a fully informed decision on the prepared topic at the time of the meeting. To accomplish this, board members are free to undertake whatever research, due diligence, or consultation is needed to inform them before the time of the meeting. This is an inclusive, consultative process that truly supports the trustees in making timely decisions as a group.

This same consultative process can be used at every level of the administration in the day-to-day life of the nonprofit. The person or group authorized, responsible, and accountable for making a decision should make that decision in an informed and timely way. This is very different from decisions being made or reviewed by a committee of the whole. There are of course going to be rare occasions when the nature of the decision is of such gravity that it needs to be made by the committee of the whole.

CONCLUSION

There is much more in the realm of governance that affects the quality of the nonprofit and the capacity for self-administration. Managing the "lovely dilemma" between the confluence and conflicts of interest and the function of disclosure; the method and practices of the trustees (whether it chooses to be a managing, strategic, or policy board) remain to be worked on by the board itself. My hope in writing this document was to set out a clear framework for the nonprofit to take its next steps. While this conceptual framework is not meant to be directive or prescriptive, it may be a basis for common language and for imagining of how an organization wants to go forward. The nonprofit will have to determine how it is going to measure progress aside from the more obvious outer "dashboard" economic/accountability measures such as balanced budgets with reserves, active programs with demand for service beyond current capacity, or the ability to raise significant funds.

Every nonprofit has to make its own governance choices in accord with its identity, mission, maturity, and strategy. Those choices are an essential part of an organization's destiny and its path of serving the public. No advisor can take an organization where it collectively does not want to go. However, I trust that this essay will serve the needs of growing nonprofits as they renew themselves and the culture they serve.

12

NEW BENCHMARKS OF FIDUCIARY PRACTICE

M uch has been made recently of Trustees' and Directors' fiduciary responsibilities. Governance is demanding, sometimes elusive, and often shifting in a world that seems in constant change. Almost all boards generally know they are fiduciaries even if they are confused by the duties of care and loyalty, and are sometimes challenged to create and sustain the distinction between governance and management. However, most boards understand and practice their fiduciary responsibility through the limited view of legal and financial matters. Though I am hesitant to over-generalize, boards tend to treat this construction of fiduciary responsibility as a matter of protection or preservation—and thus operate from a gesture of fear. Of course, there are important and nonnegotiable legal and compliance issues under the board's purview. In addition, boards are held to a standard of prudent management of fiscal resources delimited in terms of risk management. Both the legal and financial responsibilities lend themselves to this constrictive interpretation, especially when acted on as separate from, or without full consideration of, the broader umbrella of an organization's mission, purpose, and espoused values. The purpose of this essay is to recast the fiduciary function in the context of this broad umbrella and reframe how an organization practices its values in all its decisions and actions.

The origin of the word fiduciary resides in trust, faithfulness, and reliance. These are three deeply human conditions that cannot truly be defined in a court of law or through Internal Revenue Service code. These governmental agencies treat them, instead, as normative processes or what a reasonable person might be expected to do in a similar situation. The reality is that each of us determines the terms of how we place trust in another person or an organization, how we practice faith, and on whom we will rely. What matters most are the following: on whose behalf do the fiduciaries function, from where does the authority come that is placed in the hands of the governing body, and with what intention does the governing fulfill its service? Right now, in the for-profit sector, the directors of a C-corporation, for example, serve the fiduciary interests of the shareholders, and thus operate in a rather unilateral alignment of decisions and governance. The new B-corporation is an attempt to remedy this one-sidedness in favor of a more triple bottom-line approach. In the nonprofit and charitable sector, fiduciary authority is granted to the board of trustees to fulfill the stated charitable purpose by the office of attorney general of the state of incorporation, and is further conditioned by the charitable code of the Internal Revenue Service that holds public benefit as the organization's outcome.

There is another important element to the fiduciary role. That is, to serve as fiduciary means that one does not do so for private gain. This avoidance of gain means the individual and the group of trustees as a whole can make decisions free of self-interest and in line with the needs of the organization and its purpose. In this light, I would like to make the case that a true fiduciary is deeply committed to stewardship on all levels—this reaches beyond the conventional legal and financial to a more mission-based, values-based, spirit-based complexion. This could mean for example, that trustees taking a loan consider not only the interest rate, but also the nature of the community of investors and borrowers they would be joining, and whether the debt service is really mission aligned. This is a degree of consideration that reaches past taking the best deal based on organizational self-interest, to one that looks at the potential transaction in the full interdependent economic context, while considering how the organization's values as practiced in its programs can also be practiced in financial dealings. I point to this example among many because the disconnection between mission and money is prevalent in the nonprofit world. The for-profit world is not immune from this issue either, it just manifests differently.

From a certain perspective, trustees and directors stand in for or represent the whole ownership of the corporation. The sense of fiduciary stewardship I am speaking of actually redefines the concept of ownership from a materialistic perspective to a more spiritual or values-based one. Private ownership is never really separated from moral and ethical responsibilities that connect the private to the public. The natural world and the transformative capacities we bring to it through economic activity are in many ways gifts themselves, but we have lost this sense in our over-commoditized world. In this context, ownership and the fiduciary responsibilities that come with it are more an extended right of use, both time bound and transferable. How we manage that right of use, in service to what, with what awareness of the affects on the whole, with what integrity or values, and at what cost—these become the new systemic benchmarks of fiduciary practice.

This is a lot to ask of trustees and directors. Yet many of the social issues that we face in the economy today could be remedied by governing bodies applying these benchmarks, not out of fear, but rather out of affirming the missions they serve and their social value. Imagine how positive and transformative it would be if, regardless of the corporate form, fiduciary responsibility and governance were practiced in a way that recognizes the capacities of each individual in a framework of rights and agreements while meeting true economic needs. This would be a fiduciary practice for the public good that embodies and engenders trust, faithfulness, and reliance.

13

DESTINIES AND DESTINATIONS

The Values of Development Work

> *But how I'd love to speak my mind,*
> *To play the fool, to spit out truth,*
> *Send spleen to the dogs, to the devil, to hell,*
> *Take someone's arm and say, "Be so kind,*
> *I think your way lies the same as mine."*
>
> —OSIP MANDELSTAM*

This chapter is my attempt to address what an integrated and sustainable fund development program means for a not-for-profit charitable organization. This is not intended as an instruction manual, or blueprint for a development program. There are several other excellent sources for that information. Instead, these thoughts are offered as a way to examine the deeper purposes and values of development—to answer "why" rather than "how." One possible positive outcome of the exploration would be for a whole organization to embrace its development program as essential to realizing its spiritual and day-to-day mission. Another important potential result of this shift in perspective would be progress toward the organization's financial sustainability. I do not offer these thoughts on development with any prescriptive intent. Instead, it is my hope that

*   *Osip Mandelstam: 50 Poems*, *"35"* (New York: Persea, 1977), p. 76.

development programs flourish as catalysts and provocateurs of important work for the world.

My interest in addressing this topic is based upon working with and visiting more than sixty Waldorf schools and other charitable organizations over the last seven years, first as director of advisory services and now Vice President of Organizational Culture at RSF Social Finance. Prior to that I was the administrator at San Francisco Waldorf School for eight years and served on that school's board of trustees for twenty-two years. Through the range and progression of experiences as well as my long-term involvement in a single institution, I hold what I consider a privileged view of the life of organization. It is from this vantage point that I write.

OBSERVATIONS AND CURRENT CONDITIONS

Development work is deeply misunderstood in many of the organizations I have visited. The imagination of development is filled with personal and organizational "baggage" about money, power, and class. Fundraising may be seen sometimes as a necessary evil, but more often there are inadequate resources committed to the function, or it is left to volunteers. Very few nonprofits are really organized to support the success of the development function; from the perspective of those providing the program, "the real work," development is sometimes seen as a bit tainted.

The views of the trustees and the staff on financial and development-related matters are often divergent. Talking about money while recognizing the social effects of class issues is difficult in itself, no matter what the circumstances. Moreover, opportunities to have this level of discussion, which can be tender and personal, are nonexistent and often not really wanted. When the difficult conversations do happen, it is usually because the organization is in financial crisis—not the healthiest context in which to have a deeper exploration of inner attitudes about money. On several occasions I have used the phrase "wealth-resistant" to describe the nature of an organization's relation to money, the people who have it, and as a cause of the challenges for successful development work. By the affirming responses I have had to that particular phrase, I sense that I have named an uncomfortable truth. To not address this condition will certainly hinder nonprofits from receiving the level of gift support and other resources they need and deserve. Once recognized these conditions can and have been transformed through openness, dialogue, and the concerted will of the working community. However, such a culture change requires commitment, constant awareness, and healthy communication practices.

DEVELOPMENT WORK

Development work is an essential vehicle for tracking the energetic flow of the adult relationships and resources in the organization and the wider community. Understanding this statement hinges on seeing "development work" as a deep extension of human development, which I assume is at the heart of every mission-driven organization. Each of the groups of constituents and stakeholders connected with the organization, and the individuals that compromise them, requires a particular approach as their needs and interests change over time. The prevailing tendency, however wise or not, is to focus on the current users because they are so present; and, to reach proactively beyond them requires an investment of human resources to cultivate and sustain relationships and manage data.

From the development officer's point of view, that someone expressed an interest in the organization or used its services is the starting point of a relationship, a place to begin understanding something of the destiny paths of those who have sought or connected with the organization. Thus, development work is based first and foremost on interest in the life path of individual members of the community and on serving their continuing interests in the mission of the organization.

By now you are probably wondering what this has to do with raising money. Here is a true story that will help make the connection clear—in this case in an unfortunate way. On a visit to a school, I happened to be speaking with a twelfth-grade parent as she was on her way into the final all school assembly of the year. I was thanking her for taking the time to meet with me earlier in the day. She and her husband were generous donors. As we were walking, one of the teachers approached and asked if she was sad since this would likely be her last assembly at the school as this was her youngest child was about to graduate. She said that she would likely miss the school. At that moment, the teacher said (and I quote), "Well, I hope you keep your purse open for us." What had appeared to be a warm encounter turned suddenly into a rather disengaging moment. I could feel the parent chill. Inwardly, she was probably asking if she had really been seen as a purse rather than a person. Such encounters, more often on a more subtle level, are not as uncommon as one would hope. Since I work in the arena of development with many of our clients, I have heard similar kinds of experiences from the donor's perspective. I doubt any of those experiences were intentionally hurtful. Rather they indicate unspoken assumptions and unconscious judgmental perspectives that need to be worked through on an individual and organizational basis.

Development work does, in fact, address that need. A good development program unearths all of the unprocessed "stuff" around money, wealth, and lifestyle choices, among other things. It offers opportunities to process, address, and transform that stuff in the name of honesty, vulnerability, and growth, both as human being and as organization. For example, the timing of a solicitation is critical, and has to be properly prepared and conducted by the right person. It makes no sense to ask for a gift without adequate preparation and process. One test of this preparation is seeking the donor's permission to have a solicitation conversation with her or him. Without that permission, or at least an understanding of the conditions that would create permission, even the well-trained solicitor will fail because the donor is not left free.

One of the most spiritually efficient acts is to sit down face to face with someone and ask her or him for a charitable gift. At that moment, you have to be prepared to be totally open to what comes your way. When you ask for a gift, you are actually inviting donors to be fully present as who they are, with all their strengths and weaknesses, interests and questions, support and concerns. If you really just want the money and are not willing to truly meet the potential donor as a fellow human, you may or may not get a gift, but you will certainly not be engaging her or his deeper generosity. I cannot tell you the number of donors who have said, "They really only wanted my money," and "No one showed the least bit of interest in me once the gift was made." This is not a sustainable development program—instead this is a setup for donor burn-out.

Development work is about helping people connect to their money in a context free of judgment. Development work is about giving permission for people to tell their stories, to be heard, to live into their meaning. And, through telling their stories, to be accepted for who they are and what they see as possible for the world. Somewhere in that story is the linkage of values with the organization and its mission, but it will be in their language. Development work is about connecting what people really care about with a way to accomplish that vision in the world. If people recognize that what they care about is being actualized in and through the school, they will have no hesitation in financially supporting the success of the organization above and beyond the tuition within their financial capacity. The organization's success is their success. In this light, money and volunteer time are nothing more than a language for expressing what lies in the heart and is confirmed by the head.

One classic definition of branding is "a promise wrapped in experience." This transposes directly as a way to explore development work, to determine what the promise of the organization is, its ideals, its values, and then to work with the community to check in on the experience of that promise. Then a response to that expression in light of what is real and possible will close the loop. That response could include an invitation to check back in with them. If people feel engaged on this level, they will ask you how they can help—in a sense at this moment they are asking how they might give a gift rather than you having to ask for it.

This is development work. It is tremendously time consuming. It has to be done sensitively and with tact. It needs a framework and goals. It needs a systemic infrastructure and accountability. It needs to be authentic and consequential. The actual flow of gifts is nothing more than a barometer of the deeper quality of interest in others and relationship that is carried by the school.

DONORS

There is a wonderful cartoon by Gary Larson captioned "How Birds See the World." In it he shows a man, woman, and dog walking along viewed from the perspective of a bird sitting high up. On each character's head is a target. Given the language I have often heard around development, I wonder if development staff members see the world the same way as Larson's birds. I cite this cartoon because I have often heard the terminology of "targeting" donors used in development work. Imagine how you would feel if you were a walking target as in the cartoon. If you have ever been the "victim" of a bird dropping, you know the feeling of receiving that kind of attention is not pleasant in the least.

Imagine that you had just inherited a billion dollars, and that this became public information. Next, imagine that there is a whole industry (fundraising) whose existence and purpose is to relieve you of some of that wealth so that the money can be put to use for public benefit. After all, a charity would have a "right" to expect you to give some of it to them. There is no question that charitable needs are great, and that there is never enough money. Thus the industry slips into a mode of competition that encourages such language as targeting, and, even in one case that I am aware of, suspecting. Imagine again if you had inherited all that money. You can be sure that you would at minimum be on every charity's list. In other words, you have been targeted. Well, I would say that's for the birds—in homage to Gary Larson's genius.

But let me take this a step further. If I am the steward of significant wealth, I am put in the position, by all of the above, of living in a protective or defensive posture. Experienced donors have developed special antennae for this purpose just to keep themselves safe, which results in a particular kind of isolation and loneliness. The donor has to discern constantly the real interest or agenda of a person approaching them. Major donors will join other major donors because it is at least a safe harbor. Donors will continue to give because they can. Giving is connected to their inner health and recognition of a need, provided that they can do so in safety and freedom. These last two conditions require a context free of judgment and prejudice. It is essentially human to be a donor; but, in the pressure of raising money we sometimes forget that donors are human.

Generosity is an innate human characteristic, and I think every human being is a donor on some level—even if it is just helping a neighbor carry groceries. Add to this picture a definition of generosity that goes something like this: Generosity is giving before being asked. Such an act arises out of the donor's awareness of a need along with a self-assessed capacity to meet that need in some way or to some degree. There is a whole cosmology of generosity in the world's spiritual streams. Some hold that giving anonymously is the highest form; others look at the concept of tithing. These are cultural insights into and approaches to the importance of giving as part of our inner development, our soul consciousness.

Donors are each on a destiny path and are continually making choices based on deeply held values, assumptions, or desires. Donors are each on a path of discovering their intentions for the world—the way in which they want to affect the world. The work of development is to help each and every donor awake to and further her or his own philanthropic path and to support its effectiveness, both for the donor and for the world. If what you and your school's mission are accomplishing serve that effectiveness, then donors will naturally want to support the campaign or project. This is a far cry from the school having a "right" to some of their wealth. The only right is for human beings as individuals to be seen as who they are. At that moment, destiny paths can merge toward a common destination.

RECEIVING GIFTS

Part of development work is how an organization receives a gift once the relationship with the donor has been established. There are necessary procedures that need to happen in a timely manner— thank you's and donor recognition, for example. There should also be records of the donor's intention and agreements surrounding the gift. Over time as there are changes in development staff, with good records each successor will be able to build on her or his predecessor's good work. Hopefully, the donors will continue to support the mission of the school over a long period of time, and the "system" needs to hold something of their story.

One way of looking at the value of receiving a gift is to recognize something of the mystery of what happens to the gift over time. In the framework of development, receiving means serving as a steward or intermediary for the gift. A real gift results from a donor's intention to help the organization accomplish something on her or his behalf. What comes as gift money is used by the school as purchase money, a qualitative transformation. One could say the money dies as gift and is renewed as purchase money. While this monetary shift happens in a very short period of time, the intention—to support the mission, to educate countless children, to build a building that will last many years—manifests and multiplies over time without limit. Thus, the spiritual efficiency of asking for and receiving a gift brings about a generative life force through the human relationship (giver–receiver), and a death and rebirth from the perspective of the money path. This mystery, a joyous and abundant one recreated with each gift, has produced and will continue to produce a wealth of important stories in the life of the school over time.

THE DEVELOPMENT OFFICER

The search for a development officer is an opportunity to continue an educational process toward development in an organization. Such a process will deepen the organization's commitment to the success of the person and program. In addition to the necessary job description, it is a very helpful exercise for the search committee to create a profile for the position—to start to imagine some of the qualities or characteristics of preferred candidates. This has several benefits: beginning to surface expectations; developing some common understanding and agreement around them; and, knowing the right candidate when you meet her or him. Imagine being able to answer the question: what are you looking for in a development officer? No doubt you will be asked in any case—probably by a savvy candidate.

One quality I would suggest exploring with candidates is why each one is actually interested in development work or what draws the individual to it as a vocation. An organization would be fortunate to find someone who sees the value of development work as a way of sustaining the health of the whole community and further increasing the overall resources for delivering and improving programs and services. This is a gesture of service toward mission. Beware the development officer who says that she or he will come in and solve all your problems, and already has a list of ready donors in the wider community. No matter what the circumstances, an organization does not need the white knight or the rescuer in development work. It does need the listener, the builder, the communicator, the ethicist, and someone with patient tenacity.

CONCLUSION

Philanthropy is the byproduct of the following: open hearts, self-knowledge, an interest in the state of the world and its future, perceived need for and appreciation of the value of giving, accumulated wealth or available time and skills, and an awareness of the rewards of leading and serving. A healthy development program actively cultivates all of these with every member of its community. A culture of generosity requires leadership and active recognition, as well as constant inspiration and compassion. Further, the degree to which an organization truly serves the community in which it operates is the degree to which it will be able to draw upon the resources of that community to be sustainable. From the wider community's perspective, it will demonstrate an interest in supporting an organization that is essential to the community's character and wellbeing.

What motivates a donor, a gift, and joining in the work to be done for the future is deep, delicate, and unique to each person's story. However, there are some consistent qualities worth being aware of. A philanthropic gift that energizes and sustains a donor arises in freedom, the donor's inner determination to act out of her or his own wisdom and destiny. The gift actually becomes a gift when the receiver recognizes and values that wisdom, and in collaboration with the donor develops an agreement about its use. Such an agreement actually releases the donor from the gift and should include establishing the terms of accountability for it. A gift is fulfilled and transformed when it has been used to further the mission of the organization.

Brought together, all three aspects of development—the donor, the development function, and the mission of the organization—are linked in a story of entwined destinies, shared destinations, and a partnership for the benefit of the world. The development process can also radiate out into the community the inspiring values that stand behind the organization and its vision. This is the broad scope of a development program and development work—work that is essential to the sustainability of the organization and the people who have committed their lives to its success.

MONEY AND SPIRIT

Invitation

14

AN ARGUMENT FOR REDISCOVERY

Money would not exist without spirit. That is, money first occurred as a concept, which is itself a manifestation of human spiritual capacity. Money was generated out of a perceived need to materialize value through physical things, large and small, and as an evolutionary step to replace those things with a more convenient and portable form of value holder. Conceiving of money was a deep venture into social contracts and agreement making. At a later and critical part of its advent, money established equivalence and constancy in a moving world of goods and services, the economic lifeblood of creation and destruction. Based on this line of reasoning, money is a spiritual phenomenon in that the quantitative value it holds arises as a result of agreements; further, in economic terms, it represents all the work and intelligence applied to transforming human and natural resources on a global scale. Add to that another layer. What we call the value itself is essentially spiritual; that is, it remains unmeasured and invisible until it makes an appearance or reappearance at the moment of a transaction.

To understand this phenomenon, one has to peer deeply into economic processes, to see past the material to the field of human intentions, needs, capacities, and service, which are the energetic pulses—the push and pull of economic life. Money is thus a threshold, a two-way gateway from the material to the spiritual and back again. If one can experience this threshold, and the reciprocal dynamic on either side of it, then one could say that money is a foundation for spiritual experience uniquely suited to our postmodern era.

Here is a historical example. From the US perspective, the postmodern period for money began in 1971 when then President Richard M. Nixon eliminated the gold standard as a baseline for the US dollar. From that point on, all US money became fiat currency—namely it was no longer based on the value of anything physical; rather, its face value was based on the full faith of and in the US government, which issues it as legal tender. Because money was untethered from any referent commodity, it became essentially spiritual in nature—that is, its value resides in the trust integral to all the interdependent economic activity of human beings.

One aspect of the threshold experience with money arises when we are able to release the notion of money as a commodity or thing itself, and instead see through it the circulation of human intentions as expressed in economic activity. Were enough individuals able to go through this transformation, I believe we would no longer be able to live either morally or ethically with the money system as it is currently constructed.

Why does this matter?

It matters because without this reframing of money value as non-material, we can easily step into the egoistic and materialist trappings of life. The transformative work is for each of us to overcome our lower ego, and through this process find a healthier relationship to material matter. Ideally this would be a relationship in which materialism serves rather than rules. For example, the world of commerce has worked assiduously to bind our identity to things, to define us through our consumption. Instead of the fear of never enough, we could actually move in trust and the recognition of others in our economic activities.

Why does this matter?

It matters because by binding ourselves to a materialistic world-view, we lose sight of the interconnectedness of experience, interdependence in economic life, and a flexibility of soul needed to navigate between our authentic inner voice and our conditioned public voice. If each of us is to understand how we stand in economic life, we first have to understand how each piece of money reflects some aspect of our economic being, that while the money object (whether paper or coin), is a thing that we might use as we wish, it and we are embedded in a global energetic field of value produced by human activity. It is not that I control the coin, but rather that I experience humility in it as part of a larger community. From this perspective, I am its steward; it is a placeholder for all the world's natural and human resources.

Why does this matter?

We are currently using up the commonwealth (our natural and human resources) to produce private wealth. This is another framing of inequality, which is driven by a kind of pure materialism. Accumulation of private wealth is materialism's measure of success—at least in the short term. We are dehumanizing work, denaturing land, and monetizing capital, all in the extreme.

Why does this matter?

In the process of using up our natural resources for the sake of profit and excessive inequality of wealth—that is, dividing our world into winners and losers—we are also hardening our hearts to those who suffer under this reality. This process leads to a kind of sclerosis, and is actually a path of dying. Those who tell themselves they are winners because they have accumulated and retained so much money are compromising economic life for all of humankind. No matter who one is or where one lives, over time no one is immune from environmental toxins, or the presence and pressure of human suffering.

Why does this matter?

Simply put, because of my children and grandchildren—and your children, grandchildren, and great grandchildren. The choices we make around money are no different than the choices we make around values and life questions. We can be led in those choices by our inherited or environmentally cultivated assumptions about money and power, money and self-worth. Or, we can make choices that reach beyond the current money story, that do not accept the assumptions that measure and weigh money as a success indicator and an end in itself. I am constantly reminded of a comment made during a deep group conversation about money. One of the participants, who has spent over twenty years working in Hospice and has accompanied many, many people through their life's end, said the following: "In all the time I have spent with those at the end of their life, no one has ever said that they wished they had made more money." What could be a more cogent argument for transforming our relationship to money—to find the spirit in it and rediscover our humanity through it.

15

MORE ON THE INTERSECTION
OF MONEY AND SPIRIT

As I write about the intersection of money and spirit, I realize I
have been conditioned throughout my biography to consider
them as discrete, and it is thus a challenge and transformative indis-
cretion to speak of a connection. I do not think it would be fair to
characterize money and spirit as being in opposition, though they
often are. Such a polarity would dishonor the genius that devised
money in the first place. Let me make a bold statement: Money is
an inspired invention to account for and store value in order to free
up enterprising people to serve each other and communities in the
realm of economics.

As a device, money circulates so that individuals (and organizations) have the resources to bring their particular capacities into
the economy for the overall wellbeing of the community (however
one might want to define that). One result is that people's material
needs are met, but that is only the tangible part of an economy. One
might say the spirit of money lives on, not in the objects that denote
it, such as paper bills and coins, but rather in how it passes hands,
with what understanding and agreements, and through what transactional rituals.

When I look at my economic self, I imagine that my personal
inspiration—what motivates me—adds value to the circulation of

money, because of my intention of service. It is also an essential part of my process to be as sure as possible that the other party's needs are met. This requires an additional reflective, evaluative, loop-closing step in the transaction process—all of which might come under the descriptive heading of reciprocity. This transactional process goes beyond any document commemorating the agreement to a living recognition of each other and the value of the relationship. In other words, through our transactions we become part of each other's stories. This is a radically different construction of a transaction than we are conditioned to understand. And, the speed at which I am able to transact, to get done what I need, helps to perpetuate this old conditioning in which the power of money subjugates rather than frees us.

The question remains: How might we reclaim the spiritual in money (and in ourselves) at the intersection of the two? Let me recount a brief interlude I had with my son recently when he asked me for some money. As I gave him the bills, he asked if there were any strings attached. Before I launched into the whole derivation of the expression from the world of marionettes, I found myself saying, "The money has no strings attached; it is the string." This was met by the usual look of consternation. What I meant by the statement is that as money circulates; it carries with it intentions, agreements (hopefully), and a glimmer of the history of human consciousness. This string image is about what connects rather than controls or, in the case of marionettes, manipulates us. This is a picture of interdependence. Of course, one can attach "strings" to money in the form of expectations or demands, but this comes with an obligation to make those expectations transparent and for the agreements to be accepted from a place of equality. Even if we create our own currencies and exchange systems, we will never escape the necessity of multilateral agreements as a basis for circulation. Without those agreements, money holds its power in an oppressive way.

Reclaiming what is human in money and making interdependence more visible can begin with reflecting on how I can use my money in a way that increases value for all parties to the transactions. Sharing my reflections with those of others who have an interest in transforming how we work with money will help to define the intersection of money and spirit; that is, the intangible intentional aspects of transactions will then be enlivened alongside the ones traditionally quantified. Engaging in this process of increasing consciousness is worth the effort. To renegotiate one's relationship with money makes it possible to see the spirit in it.

16

WHAT DO WE DO
AT THE END OF FREE RANGE CAPITAL?

I remember singing "Home, Home on the Range" in an endless loop when I was young and wandering through the woods— probably a vestige of hearing Gene Autry crooning. The song's portrayal of roaming buffalo, deer, and antelope playing struck an imaginative chord; it was something about the free spirit, the rare occurrence of a discouraging word, and the forever-cloudless sky that felt so right. It certainly suited my privileged youth. I not only bought the myth, I got it for a song! I must have been too young to notice that, for all the manifest destiny of the open West (the only buffalo or antelope I ever saw were at the zoo), the economic and political manifestation of that destiny had nearly destroyed the First People and succeeded in partitioning the American landscape into fenced privately and governmentally owned real estate. This was nature with its integrated system disintegrated, turned into commodities to be appraised, bought, and sold according to the unnatural law of the marketplace. I now realize that the song, the state song of Kansas, was propaganda, even when it was first written in 1876. Its fantasy and jingle-like quality produced in me (and I assume in others) a lulling facade for the powerful, moneyed, and privileged who made the rules, who claimed, fenced, subdivided, and ravaged the land of America for their own gain.

After partitioning, the wild animals that had roamed, grazed, and preyed on the range were no longer free. So it was, too, for the indigenous peoples, who knew how to live within the reciprocal processes and principles they discerned from nature; they had hunted buffalo for subsistence and out of respect. They saw the military's strategy of killing off the buffalo but could not fathom, I am sure, the power of the opportunistic, market-driven frenzy that slaughtered upward of six million animals, many of which were left to rot when the bottom fell out of the market for hides and meat. This seems, in retrospect, to foreshadow of the evolution of mortgage lending, the real estate market, and now the scourge of foreclosures.

Nature is a continually evolving flow of interrelationships to which each aspect of nature contributes its particularity. In this flow, nature is like a sufficiency economy free of any market forces, one in which the currency is the vitality of growth and decay, aging and renewal, of altruistic service to other aspects.

In contrast, the paradigm of economic life operating as a marketplace, where everything can be commoditized and sold at a price, is a deeply flawed one. It assumes an endless supply of natural resources; and, it is deeply rooted in the view of ownership in which the rights of the individual trump those of the community. This paradigm is sustained by three activities: fostering the myth of economic self-interest, placing profit above ecological consequence, and accumulating capital as a primary driver toward political and cultural power. In this context money is removed from its primary function of accountancy, as a measure of the flow of value, to that of a commodity to be bought, sold and speculated with, and disconnected from any direct economic impact.

The age of free-range capital is over; not only have people, animals, and natural resources fallen to the great partitioning, but so has capital. How else can so much be under the control of so few? And we cannot really separate ourselves from the reigning paradigm unless we can find a way to create a new ethical and altruistic basis or framework from which to operate. This will require personal transformation along with the transformation of communities and the economic systems that sustain them, both locally and regionally. A first step, and this is a personal practice, is to realize just how much each of us benefits from and contributes to the commodification of modern life. If our life revolves around the marketplace of commodities, even ones we feel good about, then we have missed the entire point of our purpose for being on earth, which flows out of exercising dominion rather than domination and understanding our gifts and resources so that in serving others we may be served.

If we want to de-partition capital and return it to a measured flow that supports life and community, then the right of ownership of capital needs to transition to a practice of stewardship of capital, one that recognizes that the source of capital resides in both nature and human nature—work on the earth and the application of intelligence to that work. If we fail to invest in the renewal of both the earth and culture, then we will fail to redeem the real value of capital, and we will be left with nothing but virtual value. A living and livable system is one that recognizes and thrives on reciprocity and interdependence, as the First People knew and practiced. If we can move our economic life in this redemptive direction, a sense of levity, of uplift, may surface as counter-force to the apparent gravity of our financial transactions and the challenge of living in the material world.

I think back to my youth and the times spent mostly humming (I knew only one verse and the chorus) "Home, Home on the Range." I did not really grasp that the song is a paean to a vanquished people and land. The world looked and felt different when I was young. It's not just my age. Money has changed. Commerce has changed. How power works has changed. And it no longer works to not ask the hard questions: Whose rules? Whose agenda? Whose manifest? Whose destiny? And, then, build real interdependent community from there.

A MERCURIAL VIEW OF CAPITAL AND SPIRIT

I breathe the world in and out, and work on and in the world. I depend upon interdependence. In this sense I am connected to the peasant farmer, the Wall Street banker, the public school teacher, the factory worker, and the town clerk. I am part of all those lives because while I do my work, they do theirs. I make others' work possible as they make mine. This economic rhythm, this systolic–diastolic pulsing, is what creates the currency of capital, sometimes in the form of cash, sometimes in the form of equity, sometimes in the form of debt, sometimes in the form of gift.

We are embedded in a network of exchanges, each of which adds economic value to the energetic flow in things and services. Thus the economy lives in a mysterious way both visible and invisible, though most of what we call economic by convention surfaces in the visible. We can account for transactions; they are monetized moments. And, though we can certainly recognize the arising of needs or desires, we do not know how to account for them. They are drivers, deeply personal and also universal. Hunger is not economic, but food is. The motivation that infuses my work is not economic; the product of my work is. So we live in a pulsation between the world of the individual inspiration (spirit) and the world of goods and services (economy).

Money lives in that same dynamic between spirit and economy. Capital is a monetized expression of spirit. Its character is entirely mercurial in having the qualities of liquid and solid (liquid and illiquid assets) depending on circumstances, of being a healing and toxic substance depending upon proportion and use (equity and toxic assets), of dancing between adhesion and cohesion (expenditure and accumulation) and of moving between expansion and contraction depending upon temperature (inflation and deflation). This double nature is inherent—and necessary.

Of course mercury, the elemental metal, was named for the Roman god Mercury the latter day name for the archetype the ancient Greeks called Hermes, also named Coyote in indigenous cultures. Whatever we choose to name the archetype, it is alive today. Hermes was the trickster, the duplicitous one, the shape shifter, the disruptor, the catalyst. He could move into or adhere to other identities and through them return to his own coherence. Though he was feared and loved, unnerving and inspiring, cursed and invited, he was nonetheless a certain partner of consciousness. Through his actions he was the cause of transformation on personal and systemic levels; in his being he was the messenger of inquiry and the new.

So we live with the unanswered question: What is money? Yet money, a marker of finance, capital, and the whole of modern economic life, is absolutely essential as leverage for the evolution of consciousness. Why else would it be such a problem? Our understanding of it, our relationship to it, our management of it will either save us or destroy us. Mercury was the catalyst, the one who raised the question, created the circumstances, but it was not Mercury's task to make the choices we call mythology, history, or our own destinies.

In its mercurial "quicksilver" qualities capital moves quickly, lightly, in the force field of gravity and levity. And since capital is so linked to the transformation of thought into economic deed, it is a danger when it can move faster than thinking. When capital can be traded in algorithm-generated nanosecond transactions, it becomes not monetized spirit, but rather monetized money, a commodity rather than a currency. This machine-driven process is operating outside the framework of conscious consciousness, outside the moral compass of compassion, both guides to real human value and the recognition of spirit in the material. This is why money and capital are so complicated, so hard to understand. To further complicate matters, current accounting practice, though it strives for transparency, has no means for distinguishing between true human economic value and the virtual value created through the monetization of money—at the bottom (line) it all looks the same.

Capital holds ideation within it that originates in the human head. When a concept is brought into production in an orchestrated way, it requires capitalization (money) and, if done efficiently, generates material goods or services along with operating and surplus capital. Thus the emergence of a capitalistic economic system that naturally places far more emphasis on the application of intelligence to ordering labor and the efficiency of production, than on the quality of work, and care for human life and natural resources that are at the heart of all economic life.

"Out of the mountain of despair, a stone of hope."
Martin Luther King, Jr., Memorial, Washington DC

17

WHAT DOES MONEY HAVE TO DO WITH FREEDOM?

In honor of Dr. Martin Luther King, Jr.

> *I have the audacity to believe that peoples every-*
> *where can have three meals a day for their bodies,*
> *education and culture for their minds, and dignity,*
> *equality, and freedom for their spirits.*
> —Martin Luther King, Jr.,
> Nobel Peace Prize acceptance speech,
> Norway, 1964

Freedom is such a challenging word. It stands for a political view encompassing civil liberty; it stands in for the aspiration of the human spirit. What freedom means to me is personal. It informs how I go about the day as an individual and make my decisions, and it governs my communications and relationships as first principle—a capacity to respect the inner freedom of others even as I practice my own. Understanding what freedom means to others, as a right bestowed or limited by the state, as democratic practice, or as an inwardly determined guide to being, is fundamental to healthy relationships.

Given this brief background, I was bothered by a thought written by Harold Bloom (no relation), the esteemed author, in a recent

New York Times article entitled, "Will This Election Be the Mormon Breakthrough?" (*Sunday Review*, Nov. 13, 2011, p.6). He wrote: "Obsessed by a freedom we identify with money, we tolerate plutocracy as if it could someday be our own ecstatic solitude." If you have read the sentence a time or two, perhaps you are with me in my disturbance. Do we identify money with freedom? Is tolerance even a fair way to characterize our feelings about being ruled by the wealthy? And do we tolerate it because each of us secretly desires or imagines we could one day be wealthy enough to join the ruling class? I cannot think that participants and supporters of Occupy Wall Street share this implied aspiration. In fairness to Harold Bloom, the next sentence in the article links the experience of freedom with religious solitude. While it seemed to me either a *non sequitur* or a leap based on unspoken assumptions, the swift shift is a microcosmic example of the muddled or manipulated boundary between politics and spirit. That blurring has allowed the political to pollute the domain of the spirit, and for spirit (or religion) to be used in the name of the political. Inserting money only further complicates the mix.

How can we possibly identify money with freedom, really? Money is an emanation of the material world moved by the inner forces of need and intention. While it has many and varied forms, money is a function, not a thing; money's meaning is embedded in its service to economic life, that is to say as it supports the circulation of goods and services. When we treat it as a thing and tie our self-worth and identity to how much we have of it, we add to the complex that creates and "tolerates plutocracy," and part of the complexity that sustains it. Money is no more a commodity than freedom. One cannot have money and be free of anyone else, because money in its true function holds or marks a value that is created through our economic interdependence. Freedom serves an important role in relation to economic life but should not be mistaken as an outcome of it.

Before exploring money further, I would like to return to the boundary between freedom as it pertains to political life and the freedom associated with solitude. The democratic principle of freedom, one person one vote, is a system of governance that is the result of community agreement—such as a constitution. Democracy is essentially a nonhierarchical form in that each member of the community is an equal of the others. And, it requires an "informed citizenry" to function effectively. What exactly does this mean? It is the responsibility of individual members of the citizenry to engage in educating themselves, to develop capacities of discernment, to seek insight into the matters at hand to contribute effectively to the democratic process. It also assumes that every member of the community has the capacity, if not the desire, for self-development. This responsibility for self-development, and we each design that process for ourselves, what we each want to undertake and define as accomplishment is the evolution of individuality and the locus of spiritual freedom. This, I believe, is what Dr. King was referring to as "freedom for their spirits."

To squelch this inner freedom, to organize a society in such a way that some individuals matter more than others, especially in the body politic, translates into laming that society's economic wellbeing. What self-governed inner freedom provides the economy is people's fresh ideas and insights that can then be brought into service to the community as a way to earn a living. Each individual has a need for right livelihood to use the Buddhist phrase. It seems that this human capacity, left free, is an infinitely renewable resource for reinventing the economy, governance, and culture. But it requires trust in others and sharing of power, an education that brings us together rather than driving us ever further apart in the division of labor, and a sense that there is something more than the material world at stake. What we have not yet resolved is how to organize our society to recognize and support such a clarity of function and principle. But Dr. King certainly had the audacity to believe that we could and can. Our interdependent existence depends on it.

ASSOCIATIVE ECONOMIC TRANSACTIONS

When the old man first came to the plains there was a rolling sea of grass, and a lone tree, so the story goes, where they settled the town. They put up a few stores, facing the west and the setting sun like so many tombstones, which is quite a bit what a country store has in mind. You have the high, flat slab at the front, with a few lines of fading inscription, and then the sagging mound of the store, the contents, in the shadow behind. Later, if the town lasts, they put through some tracks, with a water tank for the whistle stop, and if it rained, now and then, they'd put up the monument. That's the way these elevators, these great plains monoliths, strike me. There's a simple reason for grain elevators, as there is for everything, but the force behind the reason, the reason for the reason, is the land and the sky. There's too much sky out here, for one thing, too much horizontal, too many lines without stops, so that the exclamation, the perpendicular, had to come. Anyone who was born and raised on the plains knows that the high false front on the Feed Store, and the white water tower, are not a question of vanity. It's a problem of being. Of knowing you are there.

—WRIGHT MORRIS, *The Home Place*

18

TOWARD AN ECONOMICS OF PLACE

A s humans, our character is formed by where we live even as we inherit the privilege of reshaping our place in our image and to our needs. Sometimes place is so much a part of us that our inner landscape, a quality of soul, mirrors the outer. Our physical environment is an inherent part of our individuality; it is part of our language, world view, diet, and relationships. Add to this the reality of the "we," whether family, community, or region—and the particularities of geography. How do these factors roll into the character and economy of place?

Let's look at the example of the Pueblo peoples and their dwelling places in New Mexico. They have continuously inhabited these places for over 3,000 years. The interior living spaces in the pueblos, such as Chaco Canyon, were very tight quarters, a kind of counterbalance to the spaciousness of the open high desert landscape. One could say that pueblo architecture itself arose out of an economy of space, the inherent structural expression of stone masonry, pole pine, and adobe—all materials in proximity. Community life was framed around the practice of culture and meeting the needs of the residents, whether that was food locally cultivated or captured, or spirit as embodied in the Kachinas. The harvest, celebrated in corn ceremonies, was an expression of spirit manifest through nature and the work of agriculture. This integrative way acknowledged the spirit in economy, the economy in community, the community in spirit. The economics of place was a reality because it would have been unimaginable for it to be any other way, and it worked. In some ways it was the work.

There was, of course, trade between pueblos. There were clear trade routes north–south and east–west connecting local to regions, yet trade was both in materials and in the spirit of gifting. The Zia, now adapted as the emblem of State of New Mexico, combines the elements of sun, the spirits of direction, the circle of culture, and the paths of trade—essence of place: spirit, organized culture, and economy.

While there is a kind of material resource logic to an economy of place, there is also a spiritual geography of place that finds its expression in how people connect to and draw strength from place, transform it according to some mysterious yet lawful interactive imperative, then proceed to create an economic life from it and in it, and are shaped by it.

However, we have organized our economies in modern life in such a way that, especially as city dwellers, we live disconnected from the natural world that so generously provides for us. Commerce, based on its market-reach imperative, has worked very hard to replace all aspects of local economies in the guise of convenience and low price. Instead, we are consumers of nature, food, and landscape, while happily producing culture. We are workers in the field of consciousness, sowing and harvesting capital; our awareness of the deeper sources of our strength—natural resources, the labor of farming, connection to spirit—is fading away. Reestablishing an economics of place has the potential for healing this disconnect, for reinstating our reciprocal relationship with the natural world that includes restorative as well as transformative processes.

FRAMING QUESTIONS

What is a place-based economy? Where and how does such an economy emerge? Out of what social need and geographic determinants? What is the relationship between the character of place and the character of the people that inhabit it? Is there value in being able to directly influence, and be influenced by, place-based economic activity? What kind of a regionalized or localized system results from a place-based approach? What is gained and what is lost in "relocalization."

These questions are fundamental to an understanding of economics from a grass-roots perspective, yet are often overridden by the homogenizing effect of globalization. One might make an assumption that all economies are place-based when considered as composed of three primary aspects—natural resources, labor, and capital. The three can only come together in the specifics of one place at one moment in time. Each intersection informs our sense of present, place, and community; yet collectively, the results of these intersections are part of a fluid global aggregation of local activity.

A second assumption is that natural resources are not in and of themselves economic. Instead they belong to the commons as it has come to be called. It is not until someone begins to transform those natural resources that they move into the economic sector. In the framework of the commons (refer to the work of the 2009 Nobel Prize winner in economics Dr. Elinor Ostrom), the issue is not ownership, but rather how it is determined who has the right to use the resources. Natural resources cannot be anything other than rooted in place, and are thus a tap root for all place-based economic activity.

AN INQUIRY INTO AN ECONOMICS OF PLACE

Two recent short passages will highlight some of the issues. The first is from the *New York Times* (October 15, 2009, p. A3) in an article titled, "Stock Exchange Shrinks as Rivals Take Over Trades," by Graham Bowley: "Once the undisputed capital of capital, the city [New York] is struggling to retain its dominance in finance as the industry globalizes. 'Wall Street' seems to be no longer a place, but a vast, worldwide network of money and information."

The second is from an essay by Wendell Berry, "Nature as Measure," reprinted in the recent collection *Bringing It to the Table* (Counterpoint: Berkeley, 2009, pp. 8–9):

> On all farms, farmers would undertake to know responsibly where they are and to "consult the genius of the place."... When we adopt nature as measure [of economic life], we require practice that is locally knowledgeable. The particular farm, that is, must not be treated as any farm. And the particular knowledge of particular places is beyond the competence of any centralized power or authority. Farming by the measure of nature, which is to say the nature of a particular place, means that farmers must tend farms that they know and love, farms small enough to know and love, using tools and methods they know and love, in company of neighbors they know and love.

The contrast between the two is intentionally stark. The point that Bowley so eloquently makes is that Wall Street has become more a reputational currency as a name for transactions that actually are happening across a decentralized global field. Of course, that reputation originated in the physical reality of activity of investment banks located on Wall Street. However, the state of market-trade technology has eliminated any need for a true physical center of gravity or action. Thus the emergence of newer smaller more flexible trading exchanges linked via the web. One could argue that something more than speed has been gained by replacing the physical marketplace with the "netspace" for conducting trade. The new media in its virtual character may be truer to the fluctuating virtual values of publicly traded stocks and derivatives than the older broker–dealer floor transactions. E-technology has also allowed for such rapid transactions that paper trails and conventional accounting techniques are no longer adequate and, even after the fact, can shed no light on the real transaction histories. Such is the levity and opacity of virtual activity, which is also disconnected from place and the accountability that comes with place. By this I mean, that when one sees a person with whom one has transacted trades day in and day out, I would hope one would feel accountable to that person or organization, and be more likely to operate ethically.

What might Wendell Berry mean by the 'genius of place' as a starting point for a measure of economy? To begin, there is a literary tradition around the Latin phrase 'genius loci' and Alexander Pope, the early-eighteenth-century British poet penned the line "Consult the genius of place in all...." in his *Epistle IV, to Richard Boyle, Earl of Burlington.* The indication here is that there is something of a character or being of place that plays a role, if one is open to it, in determining what happens in that place. On the one hand, this might not reconcile with those who hold that nature is no more that physical substances that we can measure and weigh, or that our human purpose and right is the control of nature. On the other hand, I would like to suggest that nature is full of life forces, a culture so to speak, that we are part of—we are within it as participant, not outside it as onlooker. We are in no way separate from the air we breathe, or water we drink. The logical extension of this participant stream would be to say that as we use up our natural resources we are also using ourselves up. As bizarre as this may sound, this is one way to grasp the phenomena of our current ecological condition.

So what is the character of the culture or spirit of place of which we are a part? And, how might we know it? This character is woven of many threads each of which is a study unto itself. Place has geology, latitude and longitude, prehistoric and natural history, anthropology, ecology, natural resources, energetic or magnetic properties, meteorology, and other threads that in constellation identify a place's particularity. Without looking at the tapestry woven of these threads, it is difficult to understand the economy of place. Place is in a many ways a permeably bounded system, while the economy within it is something of the interweaving or circulatory life force of materials and services in support of human endeavors that percolate within it. Place looks different, deeper, and more compelling when considered as an exercise in phenomenology. The boundaries remain permeable because excess production or population move beyond current boundaries, and new ideas, people, and needs flow in.

This approach to a picture forming, or phenomenological, process is a useful tool in understanding a place-based economy. For example, one could surmise that at its birth all economic life was place-based. Even though hunters may have traveled far to gather food, their purpose was to return home with it. Beginning in fifteenth-century Europe, with the evolution of ever more efficient transport, sophisticated weapons, and the development of mercantilism, the dominant cultures who created them also possessed the wealth to procure and a taste for what was foreign and not place-based at all—whether Africans to sell into slavery or spices from the "Spice Islands." In some ways the drive to accumulate capital, and thus political and cultural power, devalued the sense of local and regional and, even, human identity. The dislocations and ruptures of the colonial project spelled the near end of place-based economies and the wisdom that was indigenous to them. The pace of this transformation accelerated even more with the emergence of the global marketplace following World War II.

Long-sustaining village economies were subverted to produce for the world market. This conversion left (and is still leaving) local famine, poverty, and illness in the wake of global profiteering. Indonesia is a prime example. Nutritious red rice varieties were sacrificed for the more aesthetic but less nourishing exportable version of white rice.

This is a painful and oft replicated economic story to retell, and reawakening local or regional economies could feel like a wish to return to precolonial days. It is not. Instead, it is a plea to exercise our capacity to reconnect with place and its economy, to produce locally and regionally where possible, to recreate regional communication media as information exchange, to know place anew even if it is not as healthy, stable, or friendly as we might like. What is needed is re-cultivation of human wisdom connected to and within the breadth of nature. One of the greatest challenges is human encounter; interest in the other is not much celebrated these days. That wisdom will be a guide and measure (in Wendell Berry's term) to an economy of place, whether one's vocation requires working in agriculture or civiculture. The natural consequence of a deep understanding of place is an awareness of living consciously within the reciprocity and interdependence of a healthy, life-supporting, and enlivening economic life. We become where we are when we know our place in it.

19

PLACE, PRICE, AND
ASSOCIATIVE ECONOMIC PRACTICE

In response to my posting *Towards an Economics of Place*, one reader raised a very interesting issue about a closer linkage between price and place. Of course, price itself is a very complex topic, no matter whether considered in the context of place-based or global exchange. And, I think it is fair to say that even an approximation of true price will never be achieved as long as there are any externalized costs; that is, when portions of the real costs are passed off to others not part of the consumer–producer price transaction. The consequences of externalized costs are more often than not the incalculable costs of human and ecological degradation. It is no small irony that such degradation cannot be other than place-based even if on a widespread basis.

The reader's point was that it was possession of or access to capital that allowed ships to sail to distant lands to bring back whatever precious goods were desired. Those on the home front driving the marketplace were blind to the procurement methods, or the inexorable social and environmental behavior of the procurers. Those on the home front had only their desire as a guide to what price they were willing to bear; merchants were driven by the accumulation of wealth without heed of or accountability for the destructive wake left behind. One need only study Spain's war-driven lust for Aztec gold and silver in the eighteenth century to see a full, if nearly unbearable, picture of this economic reality. A lighter touch and more contemporary portrayal can be seen in Annie Leonard's "Story of Stuff,"* a short, poignant animated film about the way our current economic system works.

So the question remains about how to rethink a sustainable economic system that centers in place, has no externalized costs, and where price actually meets the basic needs of all the parties to the transactions. There are two threads to this inquiry that deserve attention. The first, to be true to chronology, is the practice of associative economics as articulated by Rudolf Steiner in his lecture cycle *Economics: The World as One Economy* (1922). The second is Jane Jacob's notion of import replacement, which she articulated in *The Economy of Cities* (1969), and again in *Cities and the Wealth of Nations* (1984). Both were innovative systems thinkers and addressed the economic reality or potential of place. Since Steiner posits price and how it is set as a key to a new economic practice, I will focus on his approach to association, and leave a fuller exploration of Jacob's concepts for a subsequent posting.

Perhaps the simplest and clearest application of associative economic practice is to be found under the heading of Community Supported Agriculture (CSA). The modern origins of this economic approach came with the development of biodynamic farming (also started by Rudolf Steiner) in the 1920s and first adopted in the US in the early 1980s. The form arose out of the question of how a farmer might make a sustainable living from his or her chosen vocation, and not be at the whim of the marketplace and the weather.

As a founding member of the first CSA west of the Mississippi (Live Power Community Farm, 1988), I would like to describe how we work with the understanding that there are other variations and interpretations practiced at other farms. However, there are some core principles that are essential to the deeper value of

---

*   Cf. http://storyofstuff.org/movies/story-of-stuff/ (checked July, 12, 2016).

the practice—especially the relationships between the farmers and member–shareholder–eaters (the community), price, and risk. Here is how it works. The farmers and some of the interested eaters gather to consider the annual budget for the farm. The farmer lays out all the costs for twelve months including seed, apprentices, housing, health insurance, transportation, maintenance, retirement funds, etc. There is often lively discussion about the elements of the budget as you may imagine, and the budget is more complicated than I have portrayed. Based upon the capacity of the garden, the farmers also determine how many families or shareholders that can reasonably grow food for. This total annual cost is divided by the number of shareholders to arrive at the cost per share.

When this amount is determined, the shareholder–eaters commit for the year and make a deposit for their share. The food actually comes over a seven-and-a-half-month period, but the farmer is actually supported for twelve months. This is a simple form of associative economics, but accomplishes many things. First, the food itself is not a commodity, because the shareholder is not paying for the food but rather for the real cost of the farmers' living and all that it takes to grow the food.

Second, the farmer's labor is not a commodity, because there is no direct way to tie the work and the farmer's winter rest to the farm's income. The farmer manages a biodiverse farm organism in which virtually all of the feed for animals is grown on the farm. Compost to renew the soil comes from the manure; the food and feed come from the soil. There are no imported inputs, no externalized costs. The farmer works constantly on building the fertility of the soil rather than thinking of the land, as in petrochemical farming, as nothing more than a vehicle to produce food. The associative form operates completely outside the market economy, it is market-free and community supported. What this also means is that the community shares the risk of the farm and the produce. The farmer will still have a means of support even if it is a bad growing season;

in fact, they will be able to make it financially to the next season when things would hopefully be better.

I have been asked how this approach is different than say a farmers market or a veggie-box subscription. Both these approaches are warmer, friendlier (and better for the farmer) versions of a commodity marketplace. While there is less intermediation between the farmer and the customer than in a typical grocery store system, it is also true that the farmer will have no income if there is no produce to sell. And how are the prices for food at the farmers market set? On what basis—what the traffic will bear?

In an associative economic model such as Community Supported Agriculture, place and price are inseparable. The community connection to the farm and farmers is fundamental. It is in many ways an economic form that parallels the organic processes in biomass compost. In the associative price-setting process, all aspects of the farm and operations—except, of course, who will do the farming—are visible and up for consideration. The multiple perspectives of the eaters and the farmers are transformed through the community dialogue process with price as the outcome—a price that reflects a market-free system warmed by care for the land and the vocation of farming. Such an associative approach is demanding of time and human effort, and not every farmer or eater can work in this way. But, the "inconvenience" of such an economic community is well worth the convening if transformation of economic practice is a heartfelt longing.

Portal #2

20

GETTING THE PRICE RIGHT

The Transformative Value of Associative Economics

T*he Price is Right* is one of the longest running television game shows in the relatively short history of the medium. The show's capacity to draw audiences, I assume, is based upon the viewer's pride in knowing the MSRP (manufacturer's suggested retail price) of everything, and then seeing if the contestants know it, too. The show capitalizes on one of the essential functions of television in that products that might normally be advertised for a hefty fee are instead featured as the content and focus of the program itself. Talk about product placement! Viewers are turned into vicarious contestants, their consumer-selves tantalized and tested. Forget that assumptions about what constitutes the right price—how it was derived, what it represents, its turnkey effect in the economy—are subsumed in the afterglow of consumer desire to acquire.

Given that the program was first broadcast in 1956, it would seem that its producers took quite seriously the following dictum from the *Art Directors Club Annual No. 34* of 1955: "It is now the business of advertising to manufacture customers in the comfort of their own homes." That defined a profound intention for commerce in the emergent medium of TV. I think it is fair to say that fifty-four years later that intention has transformed culture and extended its reach into the depths of identity formation. For a consumer culture, price is queen, not just for a day, but every day.

A manufacturer's suggested retail price, finding its source in the capitalist maxim of charging what the traffic will bear, is designed to play on the conditioned desires of the consumer. It is a positioning game show in and of itself, for which the latest manifestation is the technology-driven idea of "dynamic pricing." This behavioristic approach to price setting is charged with the need for sales, profit, and shareholder benefit. As a consequence, it tends to be devoid of concern for the costs or consequences to human and natural ecological systems.

What if, instead of being a unilaterally manipulated mystery, price setting became a social process that took into account ecological stewardship and all the needs of the people affected by it? What if a price actually could be tied to the true costs of an object's production and distribution—including real wages, environmental restoration, and other constructive supply chain practices? What might this associative price-setting process look like and how would it practiced?

One functioning and accessible example can be found in Community Supported Agriculture (CSA). Although *CSA* now refers to a wide range of financial arrangements between eaters (consumers) and farmers, it originated in Europe in the context of biodynamic farming. Further, it is significant that both the farming and the economics of it were based on Rudolf Steiner's insights and share a set of deep core values about the presence and purpose of spirit in our practical activities. In its archetypal form, a CSA is an association created between an enterprising farmer and a community committed to supporting the farmers in their vocation, with the production and distribution of food to the "shareholders" during the growing season as a byproduct of the relationship.

Digging into the assumptions lodged in this statement unearths some radical concepts about farming as a livelihood that are in many ways diametrically opposed to the way most of our food reaches our tables. First and foremost, in the association there is a direct and personal relationship between the farmers and the eaters. Second (and central to this chapter), the annual (not seasonal) share price is set by the association in conversation over the needs of the farm and farmer. The budgetary outcome must maintain and develop the farm, take care of the farmer's personal needs such as health insurance, and cover the costs of producing, harvesting, and transporting the food. The math is simple; if the total budget is $100,000 for the year and the farmer can grow enough food for 100 shares, the share will cost $1,000. The association can take this an additional step and ask if some members are able pay more so that some can pay less. The result is that the farmer is no longer at the whim or mercy of the marketplace. There are no added distribution costs; in fact, there are absolutely no externalized costs anywhere in the system.

What is created, as well, is that the association serves as a community of shared risk. If there is a drought and no food can be produced in a given season, farmers will still have the income to carry on and prepare for the next season. This is an innovative picture of sustainability in which the eater–consumer is not paying for the food, but rather providing support for the farmers so that they can both steward soil fertility and grow the food. Price and pricing are no mystery in this model. Instead the price is both right and real—the result of transparency, social engagement, long-term relationship, and the collaborative process called association.

CSA is a working successful example, and the model is transferrable to other arenas in which there are entrepreneurs who can provide products or services for a community. Mutuality is at the heart of the practice, and price serves everyone's needs, not just the manufacturer. The deep value structure in associative pricing is that as we become more effective in meeting real human needs through economic activity, the benefits of that activity will be equitable. It is appropriate to mention the rise of cooperative business practices and the rapid growth of fair trade, among other innovations, as further indicators of a fundamental shift toward a more associative view. Though differing in corporate structure, they represent multi-stakeholder community-based visions. They share the challenges of scalability and have had some successes, while recognizing the primacy of human values as essential to healthy economies.

I would ask this: What are the limits of community and enterprise working in association? And, what are the long-term consequences of not getting the price right? I am 99 and $^{44}/_{100}$ percent sure that associative economic practices could transform the way the world works with money.

21

FROM SELF-RELIANCE TO COLLABORATION

Economic Interdependence

Imagine the state I would be in if others were not growing food, making clothes, and developing the technology to publish this book. I would likely have to dig my own Victory Garden, or live as Henry David Thoreau did at Walden Pond in the nineteenth century. I would have to become self-reliant. This American Transcendentalist value runs deep in the American identity, alongside the more entrepreneurial attachment to marketplace opportunities. This could be seen as a bifurcated identity until one considers that self-reliance is linked to the freedom of spirit and individuality, whereas enterprise is tied to an economic precept that recognizes the need to meet others' material needs across the spectrum of social life. Thus, those individuals who provide solely for themselves are not economic at all. As soon as an individual begins to provide for others based upon productive capacities, one becomes an economic citizen. This does not mean that individuals leave their spirit behind; rather, they bring their spirit and their capacity for insight and innovation with them to serve others in an economy.

The relationship between individuals and economic life as a whole is complicated. For example, if what Rudolf Steiner articulates, which is simplified here, in the early twentieth century as a basic economic principle is operative—that the degree to which we are working to meet the needs of others, our own needs will be met—then Adam Smith's eighteenth-century concept of self-interest as a prime economic motivator is no longer appropriate. Smith's theory, as articulated in *The Wealth of Nations*, is an economic philosophy that lives on as myth in laissez-faire economies and, more recently, in so-called free markets. As an evolutionary stage, self-interest seems removed from what is called for now.

From an economic perspective, we live in a completely interdependent world. We can know the global economy just by looking at the labels in our clothes, but we have not yet transformed the deeper human dimensions of interdependence that would compel us to alleviate global poverty or preclude the abuse of our financial system. In some ways, the social technology of money and financial systems, reduced as they are to electronic currents (or currencies), has evolved beyond our moral and ethical capacities to work with it in a healthy way. Competition that pits me against others in search of limited resources is basically antisocial. This is the mindset, and I would say soul condition, awaiting transformation.

Consider the research of evolutionary biologist Elizabet Sahtouris. In 1997, she wrote in "The Biology of Globalization":

> The globalization of humanity is a natural, biological, evolutionary process. Yet we face an enormous crisis because the most central and important aspect of globalization—its economy—is currently being organized in a manner that so gravely violates the fundamental principles by which healthy living systems are organized that it threatens the demise of our whole civilization.*

What she is pointing to, based on her research, is that organisms achieve healthy sustainability only after they have passed through the competition stage to one of cooperation, or collaboration. Yet our economics still remains fundamentally about competition. The myth of self-interest, and the cogent arguments made for perpetuating that myth seem to ring hollow in light of Sahtouris's findings.

---

* *Perspectives on Business and Global Change*, vol. 11, no. 4, 1997.

The technology of economic collaboration, built instinctively into the fabric of intact communities, needs to be rediscovered as part of new or emergent communities. This technology depends upon understanding the strengths and weaknesses of each community member. However, here is the challenge. Our culture has taught us well (through the constructs of self-reliance and self-interest) how to project our strengths. But, it has also taught us how to protect our weaknesses, our vulnerabilities in preparing for a competitive winner-take-all economic environment. When we see our own vulnerabilities personified in others' poverty or homelessness, it can be a painful awakening. To truly collaborate with another person, no less one organization with another, to have power with the other partners requires that we acknowledge and embrace the full economy of strengths and weaknesses, and further recognize that it will call upon the power of compassion in a nonlinear exchange process. This imagination then begins to look and feel like an economics for the twenty-first century, an economics that requires new social technologies, capacities, consciousness, and means of exchange that complement the strengths and failings of our national currencies. We are not only interdependent in our economic world, but we are also thoroughly entangled in it. We need an art of economics that imagines this complex reality, and a science of economics that can comprehend the humanity in it.

22

BANKING IN PLACE

I was recently party to a conversation about agricultural systems in which "Move Your Money" was mentioned as a pressing issue. This campaign has been promulgated as a way to send a message to the big banks that their practices are unacceptable and that the values of community banking—namely knowing where your money is working and what is being made possible by it—are closer to what people really care about. One of the conversation participants, a long-time farmer from Northern Minnesota, sat patiently through the political, personal, and pecuniary energy engendered, then calmly declared, "I don't know what you are talking about!" He said this to make a point, one very real to him as there are no big banks in his area, *only* small (regional or local) banks. In agricultural regions, banks have no particular motivation to stray from their primary and productive service to their constituents.

As beautifully illustrated by the *New York Times* on March 7, 2010 in an article titled "A Banking Battleground," this is true for the majority of the United States, especially the heartland and other rural areas. The concentration of big banks is around competitive centers of capital, or places where finance itself, the use of money to make money, has replaced the transformation of natural resources as the economic base. By this I mean that the big banks have created a meta-finance system that is sometimes leveraged, sometimes disconnected from real economic and financial activity. Of course, one can argue that the big banks have contributed to developing the centers as well simply through the scale and complexity of their business. Take another look at the map and what it shows is not only mercantile centers as one would expect of the east and west coast, but also clusters around major manufacturing, commodities markets, and concentrations of high value natural resources such as gold, silver, oil, and natural gas.

Banking is a shareholder-based business, whether publicly traded or privately held. Thus the geographic concentration or dispersion of shareholders (in credit unions this would be membership) is an important indicator not only of scope, local versus global for example, but also the degree to which direct, personal relationships, and community are actually tied to the banks' financial transactions. Not surprisingly, accountability, transparency, and ethical practices follow the same path. The most important concept, and one not much written about, is that where there is a mutual structure in place—that is, all the participants share a sense of ownership and interdependence, and benefit from the organization's activities, the organization tends toward health and sustainability. In this form, the value of community outweighs the profit–greed motive, and may actually be an antidote to it.

There is no doubt that the big banks have an important function in a global space-based economy. They can manage the intricacies of currency exchanges and international trade–exchange laws, and have the technology to support tremendous volumes of capital flow. But they do *not*, and probably cannot afford to, have the values base and mind set of a place-based financial institution, one that cares about the success of the community and people it serves, and sees its profits not as an end, but as a byproduct of that service. After all, in a place-based bank, the depositors, lenders and the borrowers probably see each other at the farmer's market, religious services, bowling alleys, or movie theaters. Long-term relationships, and the natural accountability that accompanies them, are an essential part of this social, community process.

While "Move Your Money" is meant primarily to change the big bank's financial behavior, it is also creating a new awareness of the place-based banking world. As more capital stays regional, more local entrepreneurs and businesses will have access to financing from sources close to them. The result would be a resurgence of an "import replacement economy" as Jane Jacobs brilliantly framed the concept in *Cities and the Wealth of Nations* and *The Nature of Economies*. What is most fascinating to me is the opportunity for the place-based financial institutions not only to have a hand in fostering local and regional economies, but also to play an active role in encouraging a diversity of activities in those economies. The result would be a healthy risk management strategy for the banks, and more sustainable economies for the regions.

23

FROM TRANSACTION TO TRANSFORMATION

Spirit Matters in Lending

It is one thing to say that money has a spiritual dimension, to speak of it as energy or a force. It is another matter to recognize and understand how important and practical this perspective is as we act within the economy. A brief inquiry into the presence of spirit in our financial transactions is a risky venture. Nonetheless, I am compelled to take the risk because of the upside potential for transforming how we see and work money.

Consider looking at experience this way: there is what we perceive with our senses, for example a color or texture, which we could call "matter"; then, there is our interpretation of that sensation, our sympathies and antipathies, which we could call "soul" activity; then, there is recognizing within that experience something of its lasting essence, such that we might recognize another occurrence of it though it may be in a different color or form, which we could call "spiritual" activity. For example, how do we know that a loan is a loan no matter whether it is called credit or investment? Given this architecture of experience, might there be a tripartite view that clarifies and integrates matter, soul, and spirit in the realm of financial transactions? What place does each of the three take in the transactional process?

For this essay, I have chosen to focus on loans and the lending–borrowing transaction, though one could equally apply the approach to purchases and giving. What gives rise to lending is a combination of lender's available capital coupled with a need for that capital to realize an economically viable idea. One could say that the lender recognizes a borrower's entrepreneurial capacity to make good use of the money. The money passes hands, a material matter in auditing terms, as a result of an agreement, with the transaction accounted for in debits and credits, assets and liabilities. However, the process that led up to the agreement—that is, how enough trust was established between the lender and borrower to make the agreement possible—is not such a simple one. The lender and the borrower each have their conditions for trust, their deeper purposes and intentions.

Of course, transparency is a critical part of this discovery process, as are intuition, character, and social impact. The reality is that the lender and borrower are bound in relationship over the period of the loan; they have to take and maintain a long-term interest in each other, and support each other's success. This mutual trust, formalized in the loan agreement is something of the soul aspect of the loan. Imagine, lenders have made loans because the constellation of people and intentions around the loan project felt right, even if the numbers didn't quite justify the transaction.

What is the spiritual aspect of a loan? The money makes possible entrepreneurial initiative that otherwise would not have been possible; this is the essence of a healthy capital economy. The entrepreneurial initiative itself is framed by ideas that, although they may be inspired by material circumstances, are not dependent on them. And within the structures of those ideas, the entrepreneur recognizes and serves the presence of others' economic needs. This capacity for perceiving what is and what is not yet (anticipating need) demonstrates creative, imaginative, and in some cases intuitive capacities, and is why enterprise so often leads cultural transformation.

In economic thinking the spiritual world of ideas is made practical through the world of physical matter. How we find value in the world of lending is a matter of the degree to which the lender's feelings and perceptions are tuned to the intentions and capabilities of the entrepreneur. The loan transaction becomes a vessel for the shared purpose and vision of lender and borrower. Transforming how we work with loan money is catalyzed when we embrace these interpersonal relationships and recognize how the entrepreneur's work brings spiritual activity into the world.

24

FROM PRIME MOVER TO FREEDOM

Spirit Matters in Giving

If I could accomplish one change in the field of economics in this lifetime, it would be that gifts and philanthropy are understood as essential to a healthy economy, and even more so as the prime mover of all economic activity. I think I can make the case for this with two examples.

First, each of us is born into a gift economy; that is, our physical needs for nourishment and care are met through the gifts bestowed by parents without expectation of recompense. So we begin life in gift, which we then develop, through education and other life experience, into capacities to serve others and meet our own needs. From a spiritual perspective this means that what we absorb as gift, we are able to give back to the world through our own intentions and work. Of course, this is a reductionist picture, but pare away all we are conditioned to think about work and vocation, what, why, and how we get paid, and the disintegration of experience that results from the division of labor. The result is a mega-bundle of gifts and needs waiting to be orchestrated into economic circulation through capacities, needs, and relationships.

The second argument for gift as the prime mover is its necessary role in cultivating all those human gift-capacities, up to the point where they have value in the world of exchange and transactions.

The function of the intimate parental gift so essential to early life is taken up more broadly by a culture (it takes a village) in how it transfers wisdom across generations. Culture would become stultified if there were no research and development, no evolving story, no place for experimentation and failure, and no avenue for new ideas to percolate and find their way into daily life. Since such experimentation is preproduction, it naturally absorbs money rather than producing it. Education, defined through this laboratory function, will never generate profit. Quite the opposite is true. It depends upon gift to fulfill its mission of fostering human capacities and fomenting new ideas and insights.

In the real economy, the one that includes both spiritual and material dimensions, there is circulation of human and material gifts. Clearly both have value in economic terms—if you accept my argument—and they also have an interesting relationship brought into sharp focus in the field of philanthropy. Consider the following from Lewis Hyde's seminal book *The Gift: Imagination and the Erotic Life of Property*:

> Gift exchange is connected to faith because both are disinterested. Faith does not look out. No one by himself controls the cycle of gifts he participates in; each, instead, surrenders to the spirit of the gift in order for it to move. Therefore the person who gives is a person willing to abandon control. If this were not so, if the donor calculated his return, the gift would be pulled out of the whole and into the personal ego, where it loses its power. We say that a man gives faithfully when he participates disinterestedly in a circulation he does not control but which nonetheless supports his life. (p. 128)

Understanding the full dimension of this release of control is vital to the human part of gift circulation. Of course, there are the legal and tax issues that condition the circulation. Donors can only take a tax deduction if they have given up control to a qualified charity and have received no goods or services in return. That is one level of exchange, and relevant only to donors who can take advantage of the tax code. But, what about gift intention? Is that something that can really be given up or given over, even if the gift is truly released? Is this something of what Hyde refers to in the element of faith? And, what exactly might he mean by disinterested since most donors are anything but disinterested? Can one be disinterested and interested at the same time? The answer is—of course—if one looks at the spiritual dimension as one in which the gift actually carries the giver and receiver into a deeper destiny relationship (this is the interested part), and at the same time is given over for charitable purposes as determined by the receiver (this is the disinterested part).

So what arises for the donor by truly giving up control of a gift? When the donor gives up control, he, she, or they are at the same time released from the gift, freed by it. Sometimes this is expressed as a kind of relief, a feeling of wellbeing or buoyancy, and sometimes a kind of grief. These are all transformative moments—moments when, as the whirling dervishes practice in the moments of halting stillness, new insights and consciousness can happen. The deep inner knowledge and process that led up to the moment of the gift giving, up to the moment of willing release of control, is also a moment of a renewed spiritual freedom.

One metamorphic aspect of money is that when a financial gift is made to a charitable entity, that gift money is transformed very quickly into purchase money. What was "surplus" for the giver is given new life in the rapid economic circulation of the day-to-day economy. It supports the development of human capacities and a kind of spiritual freedom that is essential to the purposes of education, research, the arts, and other cultural endeavors in a free society. What a change it would be for philanthropy if it were to be practiced as an integral part of daily transactions rather than as something one does after accumulating "enough" to give away. In cultures where there is no such wealth accumulation, gift is essential to survival. Without gift, life withers; without gift, culture stagnates; without gift, economy languishes. The analysis is simple. The solution, the release of stored up wisdom and wealth—surrendering to the spirit of gift, is one critical way to recognize and engage what is desperately needed for the future.

25

THE DAY OF GIVING AND THE COMMONWEALTH

I cannot tell you how many e-mail requests I received yesterday on the annual Day of Giving. Each made the case for why I should make a charitable gift for a cause or mission, and to do so with the simple click of a "donate now" button. Giving could not be made easier—and so it should be, except that I felt suddenly on demand. As one who researches money and gifting and practices within the fundamental assumption that life itself is a gift, I found my head reeling at the unaddressed assumptions vibrating inside these virtual asks. It is not that I have any doubts about the worthy work of the organizations participating in Giving Tuesday or any doubts about the legitimacy of the requests. The state of our culture and the disparity of wealth in our society are glaring indicators that not enough gift money is moving out of private ownership and back through the economy. But, starving the beast is no way to tame it. So one could look at Giving Tuesday as a binge-feeding day, a temporary fix with raised awareness of a host of problems that need to be addressed at a much deeper and more difficult systemic level.

There is a certain marketing savvy behind the concept of Giving Tuesday. It is a little like the invention of Mother's Day or Father's Day, but with a tax-deductible twist. It does speak to the in-the-moment crowd-sourced consumer culture in which we live. And I hope that it has generated an extraordinary outpouring of gift along with a broadened and sustainable donor base. But this touches my sadness nerve—the notion of generosity generated through a one-day marketing strategy. How did generosity get so disconnected from the flow of our money and our time? When did gifting get written out of economic life such that we have to market it back in?

Giving is a way of freeing capital, liberating its power to renew and support initiative that has a public benefit, in service to the common good. But this statement assumes that if you have money, you realize that that money, currently in your possession, was made possible by your contribution (and maybe leadership) to the collective economic activity of the commonwealth—even if that money is inherited. This picture of reciprocity, if it is indeed bidirectional, nearly necessitates giving and generosity. I am compelled by the pressure to flow gift money back into the system because in the end that also supports my wellbeing. I don't control, but rather am part of. I am not a contributor, but rather a "contributary."

In the short term, let's celebrate Giving Day. It is a moment to raise awareness and popularize the importance of generosity. And while I can assuage my sadness nerve, I cannot let go of the notion of our commonwealth. Mostly our culture views the capacity to give based upon having more than enough—whether that is money or time. I would propose that the opposite is true—when one gives one experiences the reality that enough does not exist without giving. That is, giving makes us whole. My hope would be that the joy of giving on the Day of Giving begins or continues to rebuild an everyday culture of gift.

LAND AND MONEY

Panorama of Paterson Great Falls (by the author)

26

BETWEEN LAND AND MONEY

An Economic Consideration

I recently visited the newly created Paterson Great Falls National Historic Park on the Passaic River in northern New Jersey. There stands a sign inscribed with the following: "Alexander Hamilton envisioned the great potential power of these scenic falls for industrial development." Of course, this is intended as an encomium to the first Secretary of the Treasury of United States, and to the economic vision that he enacted on behalf of the hard-won and newly formed country. The Falls are magnificent, powerful expressions of natural forces. One can feel in the current an energetic transformation of the water as it falls seventy-seven feet, turns frothy white, and sends an uprush of mist and air.

The sound the Falls generate is a kind of white noise to the heavy highway traffic flowing by Paterson. Looking up from the effluence to its surroundings brought with it a chilling reminder of fallen industry in a town that the poetry of William Carlos Williams celebrated and economic history left behind.

Hamilton was an economic visionary. He saw nature as an underutilized economic resource and perceived the driving needs and opportunities of young untapped markets. Political revolution and the desire for independence constituted a seedbed for America's version of the Industrial Revolution. This drive headed the US into the interdependent web of the global marketplace. For Hamilton, fixing the major structural debt problem in postrevolutionary America's finances by stimulating industrial manufacturing was both motivator and strategy. Paterson, under Hamilton's guidance, became the first industrial park. This venture was accomplished by the Society for Establishing Useful Manufactures (S.U.M.), a private corporation founded by Hamilton in 1791 with other investors. The success of the venture was supported by a New Jersey governmental decree of local and county tax exemption in perpetuity along with the rights to hold property, re-engineer the natural waterways, and raise additional capital. Not a bad deal—it became the working model for government-driven economic development to this day—except that we are running out of natural resources to exploit. The history of S.U.M. is a bit checkered and instructive. Having supported the engineering and construction of the industrial infrastructure in harnessing the power of the river, they faltered in their actual manufacturing business and five years later became instead property manager and executor of water rights for all the ensuing industrial development. Their work amounted to collecting rents.

While Hamilton operated in the name of public service, and he did much to right the economy, private enterprise was the game. The history of Paterson's Great Falls was about new industries including textiles (especially silk), handguns, rope, continuous sheet paper, submarines, locomotives and, later, airplane engines. The industrial park along with its surrounding services, shops, and residential quarters became a place of industrial innovation and manufacture, expanding jobs suited to the skills of the influx of new workers from Europe, and was an easy access upriver economic partner to the vibrant marketplace of New York City. Well after Hamilton's time, this growth also harbored the cross-streams of cultural, economic, and political worldviews that evolved in the later stages of the Industrial Revolution. By then, the human and social consequences of capitalism were in evidence. In 1913 in Paterson, with much wealth created but in private hands, jobs created for many but at the sacrifice of worker wellbeing, there was a protracted silk factory workers' strike—it represented the voice of labor striving to find its place in the growing economy. It was an inflection point marking a downturn in Paterson's economic arc, and a reflection of how disconnected capital could become from public service in the name of profit seeking.

The sub-story to this economic development was the untaxed right granted in perpetuity to industry to use the Great Falls as an energy resource with little regard for the resource itself. With the application of capital and ingenuity, energy was extracted from the water and transformed into power, power into manufacture, manufacture into markets, markets into capital, capital into wealth, and wealth into power. This is a story of economic manifestation in which God-given abundant natural resources are seized and under the control of capital, power, and polity. This disregard for the inherent gift of nature to all and the arrogation of private and privileged rights to determine its use is a one-sided self-interested, and shortsighted economic vision. The widespread implementation of this same vision has brought us to the brink of ecological miscarriage. While the natural gravitational flow of the river is used to generate the currency we call capital or money, nothing of that value is returned to nature itself.

In the story of how natural resources are used for profit, between land (representing all natural resources) and money, is an economic paradigm in need of reassessment and intervention. They are not the same. Their sources are different, their character is different, and to quantify the capacity of the land to support life, even to call it economic, is to sell its sustaining value short. In Paterson, what all that industry returned to the water by way of manufacturing and toxic waste was far from restorative, an insult to the living water and ecosystem. Hamilton's fundamental economic assumption was an unlimited supply of raw materials and labor, inexpensive transportation and ever expanding markets. It was essentially a materialistic view, one in which the role of human beings was to dominate nature. His vision lacked any sense of or need for regeneration, and imperiously ignored any wisdom to be found with the processes of nature itself. There was, even until the mid-twentieth century, no need or incentive to consider used nature or waste as an economic resource in need of ingenuity and reinvestment. Paterson's economy held through World War II but began to fade thereafter as did much of the textile industry and manufacturing in the northeast United States. The money economy and its attendant wealth accumulation sought ever-cheaper labor and production costs, and, tragically, cared little about the waste of people and place it would leave behind.

The polluted denatured Passaic flows on as a synthetic emblematic shadow of one end of capitalism. When capital or money is extracted from nature without regard for nature's regeneration, without respect for its living system, nature is left to die. Capital moves freely about the world, across space and time; land and natural resources are rooted in place and geologic time. In a materialistic economy, time is money, and money used in this way sadly has no patience for the evolutionary pace of nature.

Hamilton's economic vision became essentially the American version of economic life. Consistent with the pattern of the wider Industrial Revolution beginning in England, his approach created the conditions that drew labor from the countryside to urban industry while diminishing the agrarian foundation that had sustained the American colonists. But, there was another imagination articulated and fought for by Thomas Jefferson as Hamilton was carrying the day. That vision was less sympathetic to the manufacturing and money economy than it was to the deep value of agriculture as the primary driver for American economic life. Jefferson's view was grounded in an ever-expanding land base that could support regional economic subsistence and produce plant-based products such as tobacco and cotton for foreign markets, especially Europe. Jefferson, a farmer himself, reaped economic benefit from agriculture aided by slave labor, and also celebrated the pedagogical value of tillage for the development of character. He understood that a good farmer is also a land steward; soil fertility and economic productivity are entwined.

Jefferson saw the expansion of the American land base as essential for more farming and agricultural product growth, access to markets, and ever-wider distribution—thus the Louisiana Purchase and the implementation of the doctrine of manifest destiny. This "destiny" was used to justify the merciless destruction of the Native American peoples, and their way of life that was reverently open land based. When the US government granted significant land tracts to soldiers who had fought in the Revolutionary war in lieu of pay (the government had no money), that land had to be parceled into ownership, measured, fenced, and priced—anathema to the ethos of land as shared commons. Those fences enclosed land and brought an end to the dynamic, reciprocal flow between humanity and nature that had long marked the economic life of Native America.

Both Hamilton and Jefferson knew the need for natural resources of all kinds would increase continually to support economic and national development. From their place in time, both could see no limits to the kind of economic growth they were imagining. And both contributed to what would become the industrialization of everything, including agriculture. The value of a human being would be measured by his or her capacity to produce economically; land itself became a store of value as well as a source of production. Land and labor were commoditized in a way that was material to all economic matters. In essence, with the emergence of property rights granted to individuals and corporations by the government, the mutuality of "ownership" in common gave way to the self-interest described so ably by Adam Smith in *The Wealth of*

Nations, first published 1776, the same year as the Declaration of Independence was signed.

Nothing in Adam Smith's text would have predicted the level of greed and manipulation that have pervaded our current financial system. Smith assumed a standard of morality in the economic sphere that was guided by the dominant religious principles of his time. But much has changed in the human psyche since then. Wealth has become a game of never enough, of winners and losers. Greed is not a modern invention, it is one of the seven deadly sins; neither is manipulation of the market for private benefit. But the scale and affects of recent events indicate an extreme disconnect between money and land to the extent that land itself accrued economic value as a storage place for money. Land is a treasury unto itself measured in ever-rising prices, which, in turn, present insurmountable barriers to access, especially for farmers.

Numerous economists have observed the cyclical patterns of boom and bust, the disparity of wealth and poverty that seem an endemic part of the industrialized and global economy. But, none has addressed it as directly as Henry George with the publication of *Progress and Poverty* in 1880. In the book, which caused no little controversy, George argued that land and natural resources should be owned in the commons, and that private ownership and the control of rents was one of the major contributing causes of impoverishment of the many at the hands of the few. As a remedy, he proposed a single tax on the value of land. This tax would return to the public the monetary resources that in some senses were sequestered in the land and in private hands. He hoped to free up enterprise and enliven the diversity of the free market by eliminating production taxes. He argued that the single land tax would provide adequate revenue for the government's needs. It was simple and brilliant, and a threat to those in power. What George was trying to do was find a monetary equivalent for decommoditizing the land, to make it in the community's interest to make sure that the land was rightfully used and stewarded for future generations. George's was a land-based economy in which the community benefited from the wealth generated by the increasing value of land. He was mostly concerned with the multiplier effect of manufacturing and production on the value, especially in cities, and less concerned about the role of land in agriculture since it was not subject to the same kind of dynamic of development.

Henry George's approach to economics represents a view that land and all natural resources are not economic unto themselves. That is, they do not enter the economic stream until someone works on that resource; the product of that work is economic. Rudolf Steiner in his lectures on Economics given in 1922 put forth a similar concept and elaborated further that this work on the land generates one kind of value. He also identified a second kind of value stream: what emerges when intelligence is applied to labor. These dynamically related principles lie at the heart of economic life, lead naturally to the division of labor, and the capacity to arrange that labor in such a way as to achieve efficiency and surplus capital. In some ways we have lost sight of the first value stream as our consciousness and technical capacities have developed. The land-based stream has been devalued as it tends toward place, and stands against the imperative of capital and global markets.

Steiner's insights into evolving economic life, which he saw as global in nature, run counter to the prevailing market money paradigm in which everything down to genetic structure is owned and commoditized. Steiner stated that all the essential elements of the economy—land, labor, and capital—were phenomena not commodities. Economic life as we experience it emerges from the interactions between them, and is embodied in people's capacities to recognize and meet each other's material needs. For example, it was an invention of industrial society to be able to attach a price to someone's work. It was as if to parse an individual's capacity into machine-like component of production. In essence, Steiner also said that capital is not a singular thing, but instead could be traced in movement through its various functions. The value of that capital would be realized in how it could serve initiative and enterprise in the economy. In his far-reaching view he felt that treating capital and money as a thing would lead to a world of speculative or virtual rather than real value.

In her study of economic life, especially in an urban environment in the late twentieth century, Jane Jacobs developed a vision of self-sustaining regional economies based upon what she called import replacement. Hers was a vision of small- to medium-scale entrepreneurs and manufacturers who would find ways to make things locally that the community needed but had gotten by importing them. Her imagination was of a vibrant diverse and interconnected economy that depends on outside inputs only in so far as they enable local innovation. She indicated that this approach would sustain the local entrepreneurship, the job market and the rest of the local economy, and at the same time reduce the environmental degradation that results from extensive transportation of goods. Her vision also includes what both Hamilton and Jefferson missed—a mindfulness of organic systems that looks at waste as an integral part of the economic whole and that finds innovative ways to transform that waste into new value. From a financial standpoint she realized that money kept in local circulation as a result of import replacement would have significant added value for the quality of community life. It should come as no surprise that her work has become a prime inspiration and philosophical framework for the local living economies movement. Jacobs crafted an economics of place in which land and regional natural resources play an important part, but her take on land itself in relation to economic value is not directly addressed.

Each of these visionary economic thinkers saw the economy as a whole system, and each brought a new perspective based upon the reality of their respective times. The purpose of narrating these various views of land and money is to tease out of them some sense of how we can actually live in a dynamic tension between the two, and to resurrect the shared reality and importance of land and natural resources, not as economic in and of themselves, but as part of a livable economic future—and before it is too late to do so. And further, to revise our understanding of capital; to the extent that it represents applied intelligence, it serves as something of a mediator, moderator, and motivator of the two.

The money economy is global. It allows for trade and the movement of manufactured goods across political boundaries, and money can move around the world at electronic speed. It supports scale and efficiency and has made the accumulation of wealth a bedfellow of unparalleled poverty. Much of that wealth is a result of enclosing and owning natural resources and newer technological infrastructure that could more rightly be considered in the commons. It was this disparity and the injustice that accompanies it that led Henry George to seek a remedy. It is not hard to see both the genius and shadows of the money economy; many of us benefit and suffer from it. It has, unfortunately, pervaded all aspects of economic life to the exclusion of other ways of being economic.

A land-based economy is by definition rooted in place, animated by its inhabitants, and conditioned by the natural resources that make up the span of its geography, however that is defined—one day's horse ride, river or mountain boundaries. Agriculture, for example, cannot be anything other than land based. In many ways, I would venture that most economies prior to the modern era and certainly prior to the ascent of the money economy worked that way. Such an economy understands and depends upon a social ethos in order to function, and every community member is valued though each has different capacities. In its ideal, it is a kind of gift economy. The Sarvodaya Movement in Sri Lanka founded by Dr. A.T. Ariyaratne is a living example. There are now some 15,000 villages practicing economic self-reliance based upon the land. Everyone is cared for, and everyone has meaningful work to contribute to the community regardless of age. They never talk about full employment as we do in Western culture. Instead they speak of full engagement. The beauty of such an economy is that the quality of community life is lifted and with it each individual. While a land-based economy may not generate such enormous wealth for individuals, it is, as in the case of Sarvodaya villages, more likely to foster a more fair economy that produces sufficiency. Of course, the risk involved in working this way is a shadow, a closed community that oppresses the life of the individual.

An example of the transformation of a land-based economy to a money-based one might help illustrate the distinction between the two economies. In Indonesia, prior to its independence following World War II, village life was very strong. The staple food crop was an indigenous variety of red rice, which provided a wide range of nutrients and supported people's wellbeing; there was little disease or starvation. Following independence, the new government wished to participate in the emerging global economy and essentially directed rice growers to cultivate white rice that could be exported to hungry markets. The government provided the necessary subsidies and support. Shortly thereafter, with a shortage of red rice for nutrition and white rice transported out of the community to the marketplace, there was a rise in disease, malnutrition, and poverty. At the same time, wealth accrued to those who controlled the marketplace, who did not live in the villages, but rather in the ports and centers of capital. This portrayal is oversimplified to make the point, but the facts remain and the circumstances are nonetheless true—and, sadly, it is not an isolated case.

In the land economy, people are connected to the food they eat, the people that grow it, and the soil in which it is grown. Land based enterprise might include food processing, crafts and manufacture from regional materials, localized energy production through wind or solar, and the list I am sure can be much longer. The point here is that the economy emerges from working on the land. This framework does not in any way limit exchange between communities because the exchange remains between people who have their own connection to the land. Because the land held in common is a source of production, and not economic in and of itself, the land economy is much less likely to have externalized costs. And, there will be more ecological consciousness as the community has to live with the consequences of its own activities. In a land economy, transparency means that a product can be traced to its sources and makers.

On the other hand, the money economy makes it possible to manufacture on a scale and with efficiency not possible at a regional level. It would be absurd, for example, to think that each region has to make its own mass transportation vehicles. One question would be whether externalized costs and other less visible human and environmental consequences of manufacturing can be accounted and paid for, and mitigated in a restorative manner.

We need both facets of the economy, but with a renewed awareness of land. By and large the land economy has been adumbrated by the money economy. Everything, it seems, has been monetized. What the Relocalization Movement, Transition Towns, Business Alliance for Local Living Economies, TimeBanks, BerkShares, Buy Fresh Buy Local, and Community Supported Agriculture, along with numerous other groups are doing, each in its own way, is trying to reawaken the local–regional economy consciousness with the rebuilding of community and resilience at the core of all initiative. In essence they are encouraging communities and individuals to take back authority as much as possible for the development of economic life out of a sense of interdependence. In some cases these groups are creating their own innovative means of exchange in order to complement the conventional money system. And the new tools are more in alignment with the values they are cultivating.

The money economy has set us in competition with one another, atomized us and left some of us in a state of fear of not having enough to take care of ourselves—all on the assumption that the only way to meet one's needs is through money. Since we are so busy trying to make money, and do not have time to do anything else, we are left with paying someone else to take care of matters. The extreme of the money economy is that we work so hard at our livelihood that we end up outsourcing our life.

The conclusion of all this economic history and analysis is to say that we need a new kind of economy, which raises the local–regional land-based on equal ground with the global, recognizes the value and role each play, and manages capital in a way that supports the interplay between them. This management component would raise community self-determination to a new level beyond politics, recognize the importance of multi-stakeholder participation and at the same time steward the intersections between local and global via larger-scale associations of stakeholders. A picture that says only one system is the answer for all, that to be economically viable and profitable, for example, everything must be built out to large-scale efficiencies, no longer works.

Both the money system, though overstretched and fraying at the edges, and land-based systems are already working, even if the latter is still surviving only in the background. However, in many cases the local or regional land-based solution is going to be far more resilient in the future because those who create it usually feel responsible and accountable for what they have co-created and accomplished. To change our economic being will require a radical reconsideration of ownership—how we own, why we own—and a major disruption of the myth of self-interest. The reality of our interdependence in economic life will have a new story that also celebrates the importance of community-interest, both local and global.

What we seriously lack to move toward this new level of economic system consciousness is an educational infrastructure that seriously challenges the current economic and money paradigm while researching and experimenting far more broadly the methodologies and benefits of the land-based economy. But nothing will happen in this direction unless each of us steps out of consumer consciousness—one endgame of the money economy—and finds a way to really reconnect with land, not as real estate, but as the gift-source of all economic life.

27

AN END TO THE AGE OF ENTITLEMENT

Land Ownership, Use, and Community Reconsidered

Ask the question: What is my purpose in this lifetime? What resounds is a picture of culture and consciousness at work in forming me. That we each have the privilege of asking ourselves such a question reveals an important aspect of what it means to be human. However, when I look about me in the world, I realize all this inquiry is meaningless without paying particular attention to the earth we all stand on and cohabit. While each of us wrestles, if we choose, with the question of purpose, we rarely ask the deeper questions about the meaning of land, our connection to it, and the reality that it is our shared commons—even though we have been conditioned not to think of it this way in Western culture.

Modern economics has parsed land in a way quite destructive and unimaginable to many indigenous cultures—certainly to America's first peoples. This market-centered methodology is founded upon a materialistic worldview that values things, commodities, and quantification above all else. Ownership of land and its attendant control has become an end in itself that has been used to justify some extraordinary means including rendering the land infertile in the pursuit of profit from it, or distorting its value by using it as a kind of root cellar for capital and generator of appreciated development value. This may seem harsh judgment, but both conditions have rendered much productive land unusable and inaccessible, either through industrial farming or overdevelopment. Both are anathema to anything like a regenerative economy. Superfund sites and real estate speculation are more a commons of economic distress in the sense that we all share the costs of their consequences. The long-standing imperative to own and control land as property has its parallel in the competitive drive for control of markets and economic life in general. This age of entitlement has to come to an end along with its destructive practices. From the perspective of the land, we are all commoners, even if we would prefer not to think of it this way.

As a counter imagination, wise stewardship of the land and natural resources upon which humanity depends might render a more mutual and compassionate interdependent community—a true commonwealth. Farmers working with high integrity sustainable practices understand this. Their ultimate purpose is building soil fertility. Land trusts are founded on the principle of protecting and stewarding land on behalf of the commons. Neither the farmer nor the land trustees treat the land as a commodity. To do so would be an abrogation of their missions and the high purpose of their service. And thankfully there are many private landowners who operate in solidarity with these principles—but not currently enough to rescue the earth from commercial abuse.

I am proposing here to recast the question of land ownership in light of two other critically important but less attended to elements, namely, use and community. Imagine these three—ownership, use, and community—as the primary elements of the human relationship to land, and, from a different perspective, the aspects of consciousness and praxis that the land is calling forth from us. Each of these elements has its particular qualities, practices, and ethic, and yet they are inseparable. Use and community are often subsumed within our concept of ownership, a situation that no longer serves the economic future in which ecological limits and the diminished capacity of land (and all natural resources) to support human needs are becoming painfully evident.

Change will require a new consciousness, one that transcends conventional polarity and dualistic thinking that are the hallmarks of the bicameral mind. Instead we will need to cultivate what was called in ancient Greece and Buddhist practice the middle way, a path that recognizes the both–and, holds the extremes of the polarity and what mediates them. This requires a certain flexibility of mind, and I would say feeling. In this threefold picture, each of the three elements are of equal importance and serve as tension holder and balance to the others. Collectively they are a unified system; each with its unique character completes the others. Like the three primary colors from which all other colors emerge, ownership, use, and community are the primary elements of a whole relational system. Although this may seem to be a highly theoretical approach, my hope here is to demonstrate quite the opposite—it is both directly practical, a bearer of collaboration rather than competition, and a possible tool for healing our centuries long violent relationship with the earth and each other. This last hope may seem arrogant and overreaching, and it is with all humility that I propose it. But I do not know how else to frame a counter imagination to the dominant paradigm of land ownership.

Ownership

Historically land ownership was invented as a right, a legalistic structure that was designed to serve power and to wrest control from what resided in the commons. The language itself—title, deed, lots or allotments, boundaries—is a reflection of the power and value structures inherent in the concept of ownership. I am reminded of a famous line delivered by baseball umpire Bill Klem when a batter complained about a pitch call: "It ain't nothin' till I call it." This is absolutist thinking driven by a kind of self-assigned divine right, the same divine right that drove manifest destiny, colonization, and the destruction of indigenous wisdom along the way—the very wisdom we now need to resurrect and cultivate with new collaborative consciousness if we are to survive on this planet.

The outcome of the present legal structure of land ownership in America is that the land itself is placed into the world of commodities, bounded, parceled, priced, and marketed, with the landowner having virtually absolute control over use. Were we to remove these artificial, self-serving, state-created aspects of ownership, we could see that there are some very positive aspects to ownership. If an individual or private entity owns the land, whether inherited or purchased, then that person's identity and destiny are connected with that land. In this light, ownership is a cultural or spiritual responsibility. The owner has a free choice to steward the land for future generations or, at the other end of the spectrum, to treat it as a commodity to sell or use without reference to community. Of course, ownership comes with the right to sell, but toward what end, and for what purpose are the significant destiny questions. The options are many, but could be looked at through the lenses of use and community as tools of discernment and guidance.

Use

Use of land is attached to the ownership of it, and the owner bears the right to determine its use, but these two concepts are not the same. The tendency is to conflate them. If I buy a residential house with land, the intent and use are clear. However somewhere in the background, unless it is contested, the use of land is governed primarily by agreements such as zoning laws and tax structures, and most notably by lease agreements if the owner is not the user. Such agreements are framed in something of an exchange in which both parties give up an element of control in order for their needs and the community's needs to be met. The contracts that arise from these agreements supersede the rights of either party, except the right to cure, renegotiate, or abrogate the agreement if the terms are not met. If I wanted to convert a residence into a business, I would likely have to seek a zoning variance by way of public hearing. Even property tax is a kind of use agreement in the sense that the right of owning in a community comes with a required financial contribution back to the community to maintain shared services such as road access, fire protection, and law enforcement. One result of this is that potential owners or businesses choose where to locate based upon the expected contribution or, in the case of businesses, tax incentives offered. Thus the use of land, regardless of ownership, is a matter of rights and agreements.

Community

In some ways community is the most complicated of the three elements to articulate, because it is the most diverse in its expressions and our culture barely holds it consciously. I have already touched on community tangentially in the use section addressing the question of taxes. Clearly taxes are set by elected or appointed officials who represent the broad interests of the community, as defined by political boundaries. Such officials serve at the will of the community. Tax levies arise not only as an expression of community agreements, but also in the framework of the economy of the community. As I mentioned, taxes are mandatory gifts and are therefore a critical component of economic life. Without shared roads, business would have a difficult time getting supplies, and then distributing manufactured goods. It is through zoning that the community indirectly chooses the best use of land, whether residential, educational, industrial. But community does not get to determine who owns private land. Instead, ownership is a product of real estate market activity. This situation has resulted, for example, in corporations or real estate speculators purchasing land and, as owners, using or developing that land for private gain without necessarily having accountability for how they have treated the land, or supported its productivity or fertility. While profit may have been extracted from the land, those profits often leave the community to go instead into distant shareholders' hands. In these circumstances, the "investor" community is delocalized from the land and has no direct or real accountability within the community of place, and, further, often drives the economic process through the free market principle of profit maximization. In this situation, the profits leave the community, but the unaccounted expense of compromised land stays as a burden to the community without recompense. Thus, the place-based economy often becomes unsustainable and non-regenerative.

The consideration of community is an important, and often ignored, element in the context of ownership and use. From the vantage point of the land, community is an economic function. The community is formed on the basis of interdependence. I may own a piece of land and lease it to a farmer. If that farmer then uses toxic chemicals that seep into the ground water and thus pollutes the watershed, the whole community bears both the consequences and the expense. Ecological economics recognizes the systemic interconnections in nature, and sees also the truth of our interdependence as humans dependent for our wellbeing upon the land, the earth, and all its natural resources. From an economic standpoint, community is inseparable from land.

Closing

Land is the foundation of economic life. The boundaries we impose upon land, the rights we confer to ourselves, are a reflection of our political life. Who we are and how we bring our labor to work on the land is a matter of culture and vocational destiny. It is important to understand that each aspect of this threefold framework must be given equal recognition and weight and yet be worked with in mindful integration with the other two—land as economic source governed by community-determined rights and right use, ownership as a path to realize stewardship responsibility as well as initiative on and from the land. If we work with this threefold framework as background to finding a renewed purpose in stewarding land rather than consuming it, economic life will shift into a more stable and sustaining modality—one of sufficiency. If we recognize and value the human community, which depends upon the land, then that community needs to have a voice in how the land is best used and renewed. The community may even have a say in who is best suited to bring their capacities to the land, whether farming, manufacturing, or development.

Such approaches exist. But to get there, the relationship between ownership, use, and community has to change, to be brought into a balanced yet dynamic relationship. The age of entitlement, which gives primacy to private land ownership through policies and laws that trump use and community, has to change. In such a skewed system, a distorted, unjust, and unsustainable system has emerged driven by extreme self-interested behavior. The world is full of evidence for this. The challenge is to develop a way of being with land that brings ownership, use, and community into dynamic equilibrium so that human nature and nature itself thrive in reciprocal nurturance.

Land trusts, the high integrity sustainable farming movement, enlightened land owners, the landless workers movement, the rise of the new peasantry, and those practicing true social finance are all striving to find this renewed relationship to land that is supportive of life, human destiny, and the collaborative community we could call the world economy.

28

A POETIC OF ECONOMICS IN AGRICULTURE

Economic life originates with the gift of land and our development of agriculture. Some may find this obvious and wonder at the purpose of the inquiry. Some may see parallels between the states of the economy and agriculture and deny any causal relationship. In any case, agriculture—bringing wisdom to the land—is critical for the ability to thrive economically on an earth whose very nature is being challenged.

A key source of my physical wellbeing lies in the nourishment I receive from the land. I know that if someone is not continually caring for the land and its vitality, it will become exhausted. And, it takes demanding labor and sensitive intelligence to coax food from the soil no matter how fertile. Applying labor and intelligence to land gives rise to economic life, particularly when, based on specialized knowledge and effective practice, the farmer provides for others. This is the simple evidence, but not enough.

To find the poetics of economics, follow the farmers to the furrow. They live the core practices through which we can see the prime virtue of economic life—interdependence. They work creatively with the confluences of mineral, plant, and animal. The farmer orchestrates the part each plays in the rhythmic woven cycles of farm life. They understand the physical phenomena of the earth, air, water, and light in order to know how to work with the life forces that animate those physical forces and how they are expressed in all aspects of the farm. Then, given success with all this, they also have to have a sense for what to do with all they have produced—the business of farming. Thus, the fertility of the soil is the farmers' enduring legacy and from which they create a living. The land is their equity, stewardship their mission.

A farmer who sees the farm as a living organism, as a self-renewing entity, and who is also able to sustain community around it, is a poet of economic understanding. She or he sees the ebb and flow, the metamorphic processes, as life itself. Food is in reality a natural byproduct of that poetic practice. Such a farmer is a rarity and an exemplar, a mediator between the spiritual and material worlds. When that farmer creates an interdependent community around that farm, such as is found in the original forms of community-supported agriculture, the farmer becomes the generator of real economic life. The reciprocal relationship between the farmer and the eaters, their mutual interest, resides in the flow between money, vocation, and production, while meeting the physical and social needs of their participants. In this model, as an eater I know the farmer, the nature of the labor and level of intelligence applied, the method of farming, the state of the soil; and, I am part of an economy that is totally free of market forces. The community is connected to the farmer and the farm through the financial support it provides and the risk it shares in the co-created system.

Anyone who has not experienced such a community-farm must be wondering which world I am living in, or which century. I am describing a way of being in connection with agriculture that is in stark contrast to an industrial agricultural system in which the farmer is instead subjected to the vagaries of the marketplace. Along with the pressures of the marketplace come all the questions of mechanical efficiency, monocrops, dependence on petrochemicals, scaling for profitability, an unstable labor force, untraceable externalized costs, and, to my mind the worst, the invisibility of the farmer in the food system. Such a scale and market-based agriculture directly correlates to the experience of disconnection from the human activity required to produce it. Food is reduced to commodity, a thing like all other things, but with a short life. Profitability trumps fertility.

Sacrificing true economic interdependence that reaches as deep as the molecules in the soil and connects them with the lives of the farm community no longer works and has led to destroying the earth. I think it would be fair to say that if we could relocate the essential purpose of farming, live in its poetic processes, we would have to rethink virtually every other aspect of our economic life. We have to start somewhere. Why not with the farmer and the source of all wellbeing?

Destiny

EPILOGUE: A CALL FOR TRANSFORMATION

In a world in which we have commodified labor, land and all natural resources, and now capital as well, why should we be surprised that democracy is also for sale? *Citizens United* has proven this point in the extreme. What has been less noticed or documented is a long-standing stealth campaign to commoditize human identity—the human ego is in many ways the last frontier of commerce. Anyone who doubts this intention should be aware of the following clarion call from the *Art Directors Club Annual No. 34* of 1955: "It is now the business of advertising to manufacture customers in the comfort of their own homes."

We cannot seek the antidote to this invasion in social isolation. Self-reflection is an important tool of self-knowledge, but self-knowledge is meaningless without the reciprocal knowledge reflected back to each of us from the world. In some ways we serve each other as awakeners and sanity checkers, and hold each other to accounts so to speak. Another way of looking at this would be that each of us needs to be free in determining a destiny path and vocation, and at the same time find meaningful work in serving others' material needs. The world of rights and agreements mediates this intersection of the individual and the material world, and the collective activity itself is what we call economics—or how we meet human material needs out of compassionate interdependence. I might venture to say that understanding and transforming how we work in the world economy, even in its most local or regional expression, is itself a threshold to restoring, preserving, or furthering the development of consciousness.

The experience of this transformation acts as preventive counterpoint to what is a kind of virtual identity theft. Money, with all its attendant issues, is nothing more than the barometric instrument of the collective we call world economy. Understand money and the current condition of humanity, and our ability to know ourselves and care for one another is visible in it, for better or worse. Truth is, unless one hews to and hides behind a protected right of privilege, the picture demands profound transformation that centers on the intersection of money and spirit. This is work that no one other than each of us can do for ourselves, and it would be even better if it were done in community, so that we can support others as they support us. If we do not rise to this challenge, we risk the human birthright and inner work of spiritual freedom and step instead onto a path of slow tyranny.